D1387374

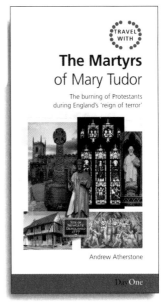

TRAVEL
WITH

The Martyrs
of Mary Tudor

The burning of Protestants
during England's 'reign of terror'

Andrew Atherstone

Day One

Series Editor: Brian H Edwards

Day One

TRAVEL WITH

The **Martyrs** of Mary Tudor

?

❶ The reign of terror begins

On 8 August 1553, the official funeral of King Edward VI took place at Westminster Abbey. Archbishop Cranmer officiated, in one of his last public acts, using the Protestant liturgy of the *Book of Common Prayer*. Meanwhile, on the other side of London, the new queen held a private requiem mass for the repose of her half-brother's soul

King Edward VI's short reign had witnessed sweeping religious changes across England and Wales. During six dramatic years, the Protestant Reformation had moved forward with speed and confidence, beginning to take root across the land. Edward's father, King Henry VIII, had begun the process of reform in the 1530s, with momentous events such as the break with the Church of Rome, the dissolution of the monasteries, and the authorization of the Bible in English for the first time. Yet Henry's support for the Reformation ran hot and cold. He managed to persecute Protestants and Roman Catholics in equal measure. Edward had none of his father's ambivalence towards the Reformation. When he came to the throne in 1547, aged just nine years old, he put his full energies into building a Protestant kingdom.

Under the guidance of Thomas Cranmer, the Archbishop of

Above: The Norman Chapel of St John the Evangelist, within the Tower of London, where a requiem mass was said for the dead king, Edward VI

Facing page: The West Front of Westminster Abbey. The gothic lower part was completed in the 13th century, but the towers, designed by Nicholas Hawksmoor, are a later addition

---

CHESTER

[map of Chester]

CHESTER RAIL STATION

CITY WALLS

1 NORTHGATE
2 ABBEY GATEWAY
3 CATHEDRAL
4 ST JOHN'S CHURCH
5 MARTYR'S MEMORIAL
6 ST MARY'S CEMETERY

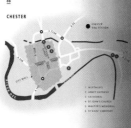

The chapel contains a fine display of Tudor heraldic glass, including the arms of Archbishop Cranmer. The Hall is open to the public, but permission is needed to use the Green Chamber.

Lancaster Castle

Lancaster Castle, Castle Hill, Lancaster
www.lancastercastle.com
☎ 01524 64998

Above: The arms of Archbishop Cranmer, in Smithills Hall chapel

Lancaster Castle occupies an impressive hilltop site, overlooking the town. It is made up of an extensive group of

historic buildings, including a Norman keep, 14th century Well Tower, and 15th century Gatehouse. Much of the castle is closed to the public, because it is still used as a Crown Court and prison. However, several parts are open, including the dungeons.

Chester Cathedral

Chester Cathedral, Chester
www.chestercathedral.com
☎ 01244 324756

Chester Cathedral was once a Benedictine

Abbey, founded in 1092. Most of the present building dates from the 13th to the 15th centuries. At the dissolution of the monasteries under Henry VIII, the abbey was closed in 1540 and became the cathedral of the newly created diocese of Chester. The Lady Chapel, where George Marsh was condemned, is beyond the high altar.

Chester City Walls

Chester is the only city in Britain which retains the complete circuit of its defensive walls. First built when the Romans founded their fortress at Chester around

AD 74, the walls have been repaired and restyled many times since. It takes between one and two hours to walk their full length (two mile three kilometres) length, although they can be joined at many points.

St John's Church, Chester

St John the Baptist Church, Little St John's Street, Chester

One of Chester's ancient churches, St John's was begun by Peter, Bishop of Mercia, in the 11th century and used as his cathedral. Near the Lord's Table is a tablet in Marsh's memory, erected in the 1860s.

Above: The remains of St Giles' Cemetery, Boughton—known as The Mount—where Marsh's ashes were buried. The cemetery was once attached to the leper hospital of St Giles, founded in the 12th century and destroyed when Cromwell's army laid siege to Chester in 1643 during the English Civil War

[obelisk image]

Above: The Memorial to George Marsh on Gallows Hill, erected in 1898. In 1989 the name was added of a Roman Catholic priest, John Plessington, who in 1679 was hanged, drawn and quartered on Gallows Hill at the time of the 'Popish Plot' to assassinate King Charles II

Above: Memorial to George Marsh in St John's Church, Chester

CONTENTS

© Day One Publications 2005   First printed 2005

A CIP record is held at The British Library   ISBN 1 84625 003 X

Published by Day One Publications Ryelands Road, Leominster, HR6 8NZ

☎ 01568 613 740 FAX 01568 611 473   email—sales@dayone.co.uk   www.dayone.co.uk   All rights reserved

Design and Art Direction: Steve Devane   Printed by Gutenberg, Malta

Dedication: For my parents, Hugh and Ruth, with thanks for their constant encouragement

Above: Seven martyrs at Smithfield, London. See page 32

Above: Thirteen martyrs at Stratford-le-Bow, London. See page 72
Below: *John Hooper at Gloucester. See page 54*

Meet the martyrs of Mary Tudor

During the reign of Queen Mary Tudor the fires of martyrdom blazed across England. In less than four years, between February 1555 and November 1558, nearly three hundred Protestant Christians were burned to death for their faith. Many also died in prison, while others were forced to go into hiding or flee into exile on the continent. Such was the ferocity of the persecution that the queen has been known ever since as 'Bloody Mary'. Her brief occupation of the throne has gone down in history as England's 'reign of terror'. Those terrible forty-five months had a profound impact upon the future direction of Christianity in the British Isles.

The vast majority who suffered, lived in the south-east of England. The worst affected areas were London, Essex, Kent, Sussex and East Anglia. Yet others died as far afield as Devon, Cheshire, south Wales and the Channel Islands. No one was safe. The martyrs came from every social class and every walk of life. Some were eminent, including four bishops and an archbishop. Sixteen were clergymen, including a number of prominent preachers. More often, those who died were unknown gentry or tradesmen. They included weavers, fishermen, tailors, barbers, upholsterers, brewers, carpenters, and agricultural labourers—often illiterate and unlearned, apart from their knowledge of Christ and their love for the Bible. One in five of the martyrs were women. There were elderly widows and teenage girls. Even a baby boy, born at the stake in Guernsey, was thrown into the flames. Those blind, frail or disabled found no leniency. To admit to Protestant convictions was now a matter of life and death.

This is the account of the martyrs of Mary Tudor.

Facing page:
Scenes of the burning of
Protestants from Foxe's Book
of Martyrs

Canterbury, and the king's two Protectors (first the Duke of Somerset, then the Duke of Northumberland), Protestant doctrines were steadily introduced into the Church of England. Leading reformers, a number of whom had been in exile under Henry VIII, were promoted to significant positions of influence. For example, the king appointed Nicholas Ridley as Bishop of London, John Hooper as Bishop of Gloucester, Robert Ferrar as Bishop of St David's and Miles Coverdale (who had been busy translating the Bible into English) as Bishop of Exeter. The aged Hugh Latimer, already in his sixties, could not be persuaded to return to his post as Bishop of Worcester, from which he had been deprived by Henry VIII, but engaged in an effective preaching ministry. Cranmer also recruited leading Protestant theologians from the continent to teach in England. Martin Bucer was appointed Regius Professor of Divinity at Cambridge and Peter Martyr held the equivalent honour at Oxford. Together these men drove forward the Reformation month by month. Ridley led the way in London, seeking to reform every area of his diocese. He appointed leading Protestant preachers, such as John Rogers and John Bradford, to significant pulpits in the city from which they could support him in the work. St Paul's Cathedral was transformed into a powerhouse of Protestant theology.

Considerable progress was made within a few short years. Cranmer's liturgical brilliance led to new reformed liturgies in

Above: *The Lady Chapel of Westminster Abbey, begun in 1503 on the orders of King Henry VII*

Above, left: Statue of Edward VI at Canterbury Cathedral

Above, right: Archbishop Cranmer

English—chiefly the *Book of Common Prayer* of 1549, much revised in 1552. It became illegal to celebrate or attend the Latin mass (on pain of heavy fines) and the Lord's Supper was introduced instead. Roman Catholic ceremonies were swept away, images were forbidden, stone altars were destroyed and replaced by wooden communion tables. Biblical preaching was encouraged by the publication of a *Book of Homilies,* which poorly educated clergy could read to their congregations. Reformation doctrine was laid down in Forty-Two Articles (the foundation of the Thirty-Nine Articles issued by the Church in the time of Elizabeth I). Clerical celibacy was abolished, and clergymen were allowed to marry for the first time.

A 'Stranger's Church' was established in London, under the care of John à Lasco, for foreign Protestant refugees suffering persecution in Roman Catholic countries on the continent.

Protestant Christianity spread through the realm and Edward was hailed as 'the young Josiah', the godly monarch who leads his people back to true worship of the living God, just as King Josiah had done in Old Testament times (2 Kings 22-23). The nation prayed for a long and prosperous reign. Yet when Edward fell fatally ill in the spring of 1553, after only six years on the throne, it seemed that these great changes might soon be reversed. If the Reformation was to continue, the king's successor must be a Protestant.

Above: Latimer preaching before Edward VI from the Privy Garden pulpit at the king's palace in Whitehall Below: Some of the leading reformers

The nine days queen

As the young king lay dying, he wrote a will changing the order of succession to the English throne. In an attempt to save the Protestant Reformation, Edward excluded his half-sisters, Lady Mary and Lady Elizabeth, and granted the crown instead to Lady Jane Grey. Jane, a great-niece of Henry VIII and daughter of the Duke of Suffolk, was known for her strong support of the Reformation. The king's Protector, Northumberland, had also arranged for her to be married to his son, Lord Guildford Dudley. This suited the power-hungry Northumberland, who would thus be father-in-law to the new queen. Like Edward, Jane was only fifteen years old. The king died of tuberculosis on 6 July 1553 and four days later Lady Jane was

John Rogers   John Hooper
Nicholas Ridley
Hugh Latimer

proclaimed queen in London. Bishop Ridley preached in her favour at St Paul's Cross (a famous pulpit in the shadow of St Paul's Cathedral), boldly declaring that neither Mary nor Elizabeth was

Left: St Paul's Cross as it was. This famous pulpit, in the shadow of St Paul's Cathedral, was demolished by order of the Long Parliament in 1643

Below: St Paul's Cross today, erected in 1905 on the site of the original pulpit

legally entitled to the throne because they were both bastards.

Mary, however, refused to submit to Queen Jane. She retreated to Framlingham Castle in Suffolk, where she could withstand a siege if necessary, and declared that she herself was queen. A wave of popular support for Mary swept the country and at Framlingham she was joined by fifteen thousand followers, many of whom were Protestants under the mistaken belief that she would uphold the Reformation in England. Northumberland left London with an army of mercenaries and marched to East Anglia to do battle, but his support melted away. In his absence from the capital, Mary was declared queen. By 19 July Jane's short reign was over and she is remembered by the pathetic nickname, 'the nine days queen'.

Mary now took swift action to consolidate her claim to the throne and to crush any signs of rebellion. Northumberland was beheaded for high treason, despite declaring on the scaffold that he had converted to the Roman Catholic faith. Lady Jane and her husband were sent to the Tower, as were Archbishop Cramer and Bishop Ridley. Other leading reformers were rounded up and thrown in prison, often on flimsy pretexts. Hooper and Coverdale

Top: The White Tower, the keep of the Tower of London, built in the 1070s

Above: *'Traitors' Gate', built by Edward I in the 1270s, the river entrance to the Tower of London*

Bradford and Rogers were arrested and charged with inciting a riot at St Paul's Cross during a pro-Catholic sermon. In fact they had succeeded in quelling the disturbance and had protected the preacher when someone in the crowd threw a dagger at him, but they were imprisoned nonetheless. Meanwhile various opponents of the Reformation, who had been imprisoned under Edward VI, were set free. Bishop Stephen Gardiner, a long-time antagonist of Archbishop Cranmer, was released from the Tower and appointed Lord Chancellor.

In November 1553 Lady Jane was put on trial for treason at London's Guildhall. Accused alongside her were Archbishop Cranmer, the Duke of Suffolk, Guildford Dudley and Dudley's two brothers. The prisoners were forced to march from the Tower to the Guildhall, with an axe leading the procession, to show the kind of death they would suffer. All the defendants pleaded guilty and were condemned to death, although the sentences were not carried out immediately.

Meanwhile on mainland Europe, Charles V (King of Spain and Holy Roman Emperor) had plans to marry his son, Prince Philip, to Queen Mary. Philip was not only a staunch Roman Catholic, but also a foreigner. As a result, in January 1554 Sir Thomas Wyatt organized a rebellion in Kent against this 'Spanish Match'. Wyatt marched

were arrested, apparently for a debt they owed to the queen. Latimer was dragged from quiet retirement in a Leicestershire village and sent to the Tower.

Above: London's Guildhall, where Cranmer stood trial for treason

Below: The head of the Duke of Suffolk, father of Lady Jane Grey. It was found in 1851 in a small vault at Holy Trinity Minories (near Tower Hill) and kept in a glass box for many decades, but has since been reburied

to London with his army, but once again there was a wave of popular support in Mary's favour. The rebels were defeated in battle a mile outside Westminster (in what is now Hyde Park) and the queen became even more severe against those she saw as a threat to her power. Wyatt and a hundred of his followers were executed. Lady Elizabeth was arrested and placed in the Tower. Lady Jane Grey was sent to the block with her husband and father. Archbishop Cranmer, however, was preserved. The queen thought his treason against God was worse than his treason against the crown, and wanted him tried for heresy.

The Reformation undone

Piece by piece, Mary began to undo the Protestant Reformation that had been established in England under her half-brother. In August 1553 all preaching was banned, except by the queen's licence. In October, Convocation (a synod of bishops and senior

The reformers were agreed that no Christian is obliged to face persecution if there is an opportunity to escape without denying Christ. As they observed, Jesus Christ himself instructed his followers: 'When they persecute you in one town, flee to the next ...' (Matthew 10:23).

When the persecution of Protestants began in England in 1553, some chose to face it, even though that meant likely death. Others, however, managed to go into hiding or flee abroad. During Mary's reign, about eight hundred people sought refuge on the continent. Some found hospitality with leading continental reformers, such as John Calvin at Geneva or Henry Bullinger at Zurich. Others settled in Frankfurt, Strassburg (modern day Strasbourg), Emden, Basel and elsewhere. There they formed active English communities, circulating Protestant literature and seeking to encourage their brethren at home. Amongst those able to escape were John Ponet (Bishop of Winchester), William Barlow (Bishop of Bath and Wells) and John Scory (Bishop of Chichester). Miles Coverdale (Bishop of Exeter and Bible translator) was captured and was an obvious candidate for the stake, but King Christian III, the Protestant King of Denmark, intervened on his behalf. Queen Mary, not wanting to damage trade between England and the Danes, allowed Coverdale to go into exile.

Many of the exiles returned home after Queen Mary's death to

become leaders in the English Church. These included Edmund Grindal (later Archbishop of Canterbury), Edwin Sandys (later Archbishop of York), John Jewell (later Bishop of Salisbury), James Pilkington (later Bishop of Durham) and Richard Cox (later Bishop of Ely). John Knox, who took refuge in Geneva and Frankfurt, returned to become leader of the Reformation in Scotland (see the Day One Travel Guide, *Travel with John Knox* by David Campbell).

clergy) declared the doctrine of transubstantiation to be true (see box page 18: 'The issues at stake'). In December, Parliament repealed the Act of Uniformity and all other Protestant legislation which had been passed under Edward VI. Church services reverted from English to Latin. The *Book of Common Prayer* was declared illegal and the mass restored. Roman Catholic ceremonies

Above: Latimer, Ridley, Cranmer and Bradford in the Tower of London. As a result of Wyatt's rebellion, the Tower filled up with new prisoners and the reformers were glad to share a cell, where they could pray and study together

began to reappear—there were soon processions through the streets, priests reverted to medieval vestments and the tonsure (shaving part of their heads), altars were substituted for tables, images of saints were re-hung, holy bread, holy water and holy days were reinstated. Protestant books were confiscated and burned. Those Protestant clergy who had not yet been arrested were removed and replaced by others sympathetic to the religion of Rome.

In March 1554 the queen restored clerical celibacy and commanded that all married clergy be deprived of their benefices. A tenth of the clergy had wed in the reign of Edward VI, but if they did not now throw their wives and children out of their homes, they would themselves be thrown out of their parishes. Protestant ministers appeared at the Court of Arches (the highest ecclesiastical court in the land) to defend their marriages as allowed by Scripture and early church practice, but to no avail. Meanwhile Mary closed the 'Stranger's Church' and expelled all the foreign Protestants from London. When their ships reached the continent, the Roman Catholic authorities were often waiting there to arrest them. Peter Martyr was imprisoned for six months before being allowed to escape to Strassburg. His wife, however, had died in Oxford in 1553 and her body was later exhumed and publicly burned.

Remembering the martyrs: John Foxe

One of the exiles of Mary's reign was John Foxe, a clergyman from London. During the reign of Edward VI, he began to write about the sufferings of Protestant martyrs over the previous one hundred and forty-five years, from William Sawtrey in 1401 to Anne Askew in 1546. When Mary came to the throne, Foxe escaped to the continent with his manuscript and published it in Latin as *Rerum in Ecclesia Gestarum* ('Church Affairs'). During his exile, he collected as much information as he could about the new martyrs and continued these researches when he returned to England in October 1559. Foxe travelled around the country to interview eye-witnesses, examine church archives and copy martyrs' letters and statements. An English version of his martyrology, taking the story up to the death of Mary Tudor, appeared in 1563 entitled *Acts and Monuments of These Latter and Perilous Days*. A second and much expanded edition came out in 1570, running to 2,335 pages and 3,150,000 words. It is nearly four times the length of the Bible and the longest single work ever published in the English language. It soon became known as Foxe's *Book of Martyrs* and inspired generations of readers with its account of the sufferings and fortitude of its Protestant heroes.

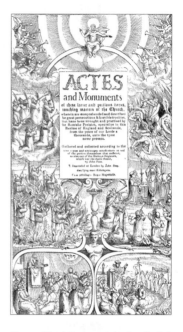

Above: *The title-page of the first English edition of* Foxe's Book of Martyrs *summarizes his message. On the left are the godly, worshipping the Lord, studying their Bibles and being burned at the stake. On the right are the ungodly, worshipping the consecrated bread, saying the rosary and going in ritual procession*

Below: *John Foxe*

Left: Plaque at Great St Mary's in Cambridge, commemorating the exhumation and burning of Professor Martin Bucer's body in 1557

The same fate befell Bucer's body, he having died in Cambridge in 1551. In the run-up to Easter 1554 there was a fresh wave of arrests as courageous Protestants demonstrated against the reintroduction of Roman Catholic practices during Lent and 'Holy Week'. In April the three most prominent prisoners—Cranmer, Latimer and Ridley—were sent down from the Tower of London to Oxford to take part in a theological 'disputation' before the University. This was no more than a show trial, intended to humiliate the reformers and discredit their teaching, and ended in the three men being declared guilty of 'heresy' and excommunicated.

By the end of 1554 all was ready for England to be received back into fellowship with the Church of Rome, after twenty years of hostility. Cardinal Reginald Pole had been in lengthy exile on the continent and he was now sent back to England as legate (representative) of Pope Julius III to absolve Parliament of 'all heresy and schism'. On the last day of November, amidst scenes of great jubilation, Pole pronounced the realm reconciled with the See of Rome and the schism begun by Henry VIII formally at an end. He declared that 30 November should be kept as a great festival, the Feast of the Reconciliation, for all time. For the reformers, however, worse was still to come.

Above: The Bloody Tower, within the Tower of London, where Cranmer was imprisoned

The issues at stake

At the heart of the teaching of the Reformation lay two great affirmations: *sola fide* ('faith alone') and *sola scriptura* ('scripture alone'). The reformers believed that forgiveness of sins and eternal life comes through faith alone in Christ alone. It is a completely free gift from God, received by grace alone and not earned by human merit or church ceremony. The reformers insisted that Christ is the only Saviour and the only Mediator between humanity and God, not the church and its clergy, nor the Virgin Mary and the saints. Furthermore, they maintained that the final authority in matters of faith and conduct is not the Pope or church councils or Christian tradition, but the Bible alone—the infallible and all-sufficient word of God. These were the central convictions of the Reformation, having been distorted and forgotten by the medieval church.

The Protestants arrested by Queen Mary's officials often had to defend their adherence to these essential doctrines of the reformed faith. In almost every case, however, the particular issue about which they were interrogated was the doctrine of transubstantiation. This Roman Catholic dogma declared that the consecrated bread and wine at the mass became literally the body and blood of Christ—that Christ was 'corporeally', rather than 'spiritually', present in the sacramental elements. The reformers believed that this doctrine was not just an argument about words, but that it struck at the very root of the Christian gospel itself. For almost all of the Marian martyrs, their life or death hinged upon their view of the mass. It became the key test of orthodoxy.

According to the reformers, the doctrine of transubstantiation has four serious consequences:

i) It undermines Christ's finished work on the cross. A sacrifice which needs to be repeated is not perfect and complete.

ii) It undermines Christ's priestly office. Sinful men are raised into the position of mediators between God and man, and the Great High Priest is robbed of his glory.

iii) It undermines Christ's humanity. If Christ has a real human body, it cannot be in more than one place at the same time.

iv) It encourages idolatry. Bread and wine are venerated and worshipped as God.

For these reasons, the Protestants in Mary's reign thought it better to be burned alive than to subscribe to the doctrine of transubstantiation. In their view, the Christian gospel was at issue.

Pictured: *The medal struck to celebrate the return of England to Roman Catholicism. The kneeling figure represents England, being raised to her feet by Pope Julius III. Looking on are Cardinal Pole, Emperor Charles V, Philip II and Queen Mary*

Left: St Paul's, designed by Sir Christopher Wren after the Great Fire in 1666, seen from the Millennium Bridge

TRAVEL INFORMATION

St Paul's Cathedral

St Paul's Cathedral, London, EC4
www.stpauls.co.uk

Above: Old St Paul's as it was. The spire burned down in 1561 and the whole cathedral in the Great Fire of 1666. At the south-west corner stands the Lollards' Tower, the private gaol of the Bishop of London, where a number of Protestants were imprisoned

A cathedral dedicated to St Paul has overlooked the City of London since AD 604, although the first buildings were burned down or sacked by the Vikings. After the Norman Conquest of Britain, a new cathedral was begun in 1087 and took more than two centuries to complete. It was burned down in the Great Fire of 1666 in which two-thirds of the City of London was destroyed, including 13,200 houses, eighty-seven parish churches and old St Paul's. New St Paul's, with its famous dome, was designed by Sir Christopher Wren and built between 1675 and 1710.

The Guildhall

The Guildhall, Gresham
Street, London, EC2
www.cityoflondon.
gov.uk
☎ 020 7606 3030

The Guildhall has been
the administrative
centre of the City of
London for more than
eight hundred years.
Major trials used to take
place here, such as those
of Anne Askew, Lady Jane
Grey and Archbishop
Cranmer. The Great Hall
and large medieval crypt
date back to 1411 and
survived both the Great
Fire of London and the
Second World War Blitz.

Above: *Interior, The Guildhall*

Above: *The crypt of St Mary-le-Bow in London, with bow arches, which gave the Court of Arches its name*

The Court of Arches

St Mary-le-Bow,
Cheapside, London, EC2
www.stmarylebow.co.uk
☎ 020 7248 5139

St Mary-le-Bow (or Bow Church) takes its name from the bow arches of its 11th century crypt. This crypt also gave its name to the Court of Arches, the most important ecclesiastical court in England, which met here from the early Middle Ages. The church was destroyed by the Great Fire of London, rebuilt by Sir Christopher Wren and subsequently bombed in the Second World War.

Above: The Beauchamp Tower, built in 1281, part of the Tower of London and home to many of its high-ranking prisoners. Lady Jane Grey's name can still be seen where it was carved on the walls by her husband, Lord Dudley

Above: The steeple of St Mary-le-Bow, built by Sir Christopher Wren in 1672. Traditionally, only those born within the sound of the Bow bells can claim to be true Londoners or 'Cockneys'

The Tower of London

The Tower of London,
Tower Hill, London, EC3
www.hrp.org.uk
☎ 0870 756 6060

William the Conqueror began to build the Tower of London in 1067, soon after the Battle of Hastings. It is now a large complex of fortifications and houses the Crown Jewels. The Tower ceased to be a royal residence under Henry VIII in the 1530s, but continued to function as a state prison until the 1940s. Lady Jane Grey was beheaded on Tower Green in 1554 and the male members of her family on Tower Hill. They are buried in the Chapel Royal of St Peter ad Vincula.

Westminster Abbey

Westminster Abbey,
London, SW1
www.westminster-abbey.org
☎ 020 7222 5152

Westminster Abbey began as a Benedictine monastery, endowed by Edward the Confessor, the last Anglo-Saxon king. It was pulled down in the middle of the 13th century by Henry III, who erected the present building. Every coronation since that of William the Conqueror in 1066 has been held here, as well as numerous other royal events. There are many tombs of kings and queens, as well as countless memorials to the great and the famous.

Above: One wall, with its 14th century rose window, is all that remains from the Bishop of Winchester's palace in Southwark. His private prison, the Clink, stood nearby

St Mary Overie in Southwark (now Southwark Cathedral). The most high-profile prisoners were again interrogated, excommunicated and formally condemned as 'heretics'. By this swift action the authorities hoped either to prove the weakness of the Protestant leaders and thus discredit them, or else to terrify the rank and file into submission. When they heard the death sentence, the martyrs joyfully gave thanks to God and rebuked the gathered bishops: 'We do not doubt that God the Righteous Judge will require our blood at your hands, and the proudest of you will regret your return to antichrist and the tyranny that you now show against the flock of Christ.'

It was government policy to burn the condemned men in the towns where they had once lived and preached, as a warning to the local populace. Over the next few days, John Rogers was burned in London within sight of his parish church. Laurence Saunders was sent back to Coventry, John Hooper to Gloucester, Rowland Taylor to Hadleigh, Robert Ferrar to Carmarthen. There were also plans to send John Bradford back to Manchester. Soon the fires of persecution were blazing across England and Wales.

The ice is broken

On Monday morning, 4 February 1555, John Rogers was woken from a deep sleep in his prison cell by the gaoler's wife and told to dress quickly. He was one of London's leading preachers and had previously worked on the continent in Bible translation, alongside William Tyndale and Miles Coverdale. He had been the Roman Catholic priest at the English House in Antwerp, but Tyndale's witness led him to embrace the Protestant faith. Rogers was compiler of the 1537 *Matthew's Bible*, the first English version licensed by Henry VIII. He was now about to inherit the martyrs' mantle from Tyndale by becoming the first Protestant to be burned in Queen Mary's reign. Asked if he would revoke his views on the sacraments, Rogers replied, 'That which I have preached, I will seal with my

Above: *The reredos at Southwark Cathedral, erected in 1905. The statue in the bottom row, on the extreme left, is that of John Rogers, also shown in detail*

blood.' So he was led out from Newgate prison and passed his old church, to nearby Smithfield market. The streets were thronged with people, though he was forbidden to address them. Instead he recited Psalm 51 as he walked and the onlookers were amazed by his courage. Count Noailles, the French Ambassador, later wrote that this martyr went to his death 'as if he had been led to a wedding'. Standing in the crowd were Rogers' wife and eleven children, with whom he had been allowed no contact for many months. The family managed only a few brief words before Rogers was forced onwards.

Above: *The goddess Justicia stands atop the Old Bailey, on the site of Newgate prison*

The stake was set up at Smithfield a few yards from St Bartholomew's priory. As the fire took hold, Rogers washed his hands in the flame 'as if it had been cold water'. He then lifted up his hands to heaven and remained

THE CORPORATION OF
SITE OF
NEWGATE
DEMOLISHED
1777
THE CITY OF LONDON

Mary Tudor was not the first English monarch to have her subjects burned for their religious views, nor the last. In 1555 she revived the infamous Parliamentary Act of 1401, *De Haeretico Comburendo* ('On the Burning of Heretics'), which had allowed for the ruthless persecution of Lollards in the early 15th century. In the early 16th century, about forty people were burned to death during Henry VIII's reign. Lollards were burned at Amersham, Coventry and elsewhere in the 1510s and 20s, and a large group of Dutch Anabaptists at London in 1535. Other early Protestant preachers were burned at Smithfield, such as John Frith (in 1533), Robert Barnes (in 1540) and Anne Askew (in 1546). Henry VIII's Act of Six Articles (1539), known to the reformers as 'the whip with six strings', restored much Roman Catholic teaching and allowed for the burning of those who rejected the doctrine of transubstantiation.

It was taken for granted across Europe, by both Protestants and Roman Catholics, that burning was an appropriate punishment for heresy. In Calvin's Geneva, Michael Servetus was notoriously burned to death in 1553 for denying the Trinity. Similarly in England, Edward VI had Joan Boucher (or 'Joan of Kent') and George van Parris burned at Smithfield for their heretical views of Christ, with the support of the Protestant bishops. Likewise Queen Elizabeth sent two radical Anabaptists to the stake. The last people to be burned in England for heresy were Bartholomew Legate (at Smithfield) and Edward Wightman (at Lichfield). They died in 1612, under James I, for denying the Trinity.

Between 1577 and 1603, Elizabeth also executed one hundred and eighty-three Roman Catholics (one hundred and twenty-three of them priests). Many were hanged, drawn and quartered at Tyburn for high treason—for conspiracy to have the queen assassinated or deposed. By contrast, the Protestant martyrs under Mary were noted for their loyalty to the crown.

in that attitude of prayer until death came. A flock of doves happened to fly overhead and some said that one of the doves was the Holy Spirit come to take the martyr to heaven. Four days later, Bradford wrote to Cranmer, Latimer and Ridley at Oxford: 'Our dear brother Rogers has broken the ice valiantly.' Before the year was over, Smithfield had claimed the lives of many other supporters of the Reformation, such as John Cardmaker, John Philpot and John Bradford himself. 'Smithfield' was soon to become a byword for bloody persecution.

A waverer stands firm

John Cardmaker began his career as a Roman Catholic friar, but

after the dissolution of the monasteries he became a Protestant minister. During Edward VI's reign he was appointed prebendary and chancellor of Wells cathedral, and preacher at St Paul's cathedral, where he exercised an influential ministry. When the persecution began, Cardmaker and his bishop (William Barlow, Bishop of Bath and Wells) disguised themselves as servants and attempted to flee to the continent. They were arrested and thrown into the Fleet prison before being put on trial at St Mary Overie in Southwark in January 1555. Surprisingly their answers under examination were found acceptable. Whether their Christian convictions melted in the face of the death penalty or whether the authorities wanted to claim high profile recantations for the purpose of propaganda, is unclear. Barlow was allowed to escape to Germany and returned after Mary's death to become Bishop of Chichester. Edmund Bonner, Bishop of London, told the public that Cardmaker would also soon be released after he had subscribed to various articles on

Above: *John Rogers washes his hands in the flame, from Foxe's* Book of Martyrs

Top: *St Sepulchre-without-Newgate, near Smithfield, where John Rogers was rector*

Above: The 13th century gateway of the priory church of St Bartholomew the Great, which overlooks Smithfield

conversation with the sheriffs, which made the onlookers think he was about to recant. He knelt down to pray, but still fully clothed, which only confirmed their suspicions. At last Cardmaker got up, stripped down to his shirt, walked to the stake and kissed it. He took Warne by the hand and encouraged him, and then gave himself to be chained. At this the crowd shouted for joy: 'God be praised! The Lord strengthen you, Cardmaker! The Lord Jesus receive your spirit!' Then the fires were lit. Warne's widow, Elizabeth, was burned at Stratford-le-Bow in Essex three months later.

O England, repent!

John Bradford was another of London's leading preachers, who had been singled out by Ridley as a future bishop—an appointment prevented only by the death of the king. In January 1555 he was condemned to death along with the other reformers at St Mary Overie in Southwark. When Gardiner read the order of excommunication, Bradford fell down on his knees and thanked God that he had been counted worthy to suffer for his name's sake. He was returned to the Poultry Compter (a small prison), and kept in close confinement waiting an early execution. As his friends and colleagues were burned one by one in the first weeks of February, Bradford expected to die with them.

transubstantiation. However, encouraged by his fellow prisoners, he stood by his Protestant convictions, laying them out fully in arguments with Roman Catholic theologians and in written answers to Bonner's questions. These were enough to condemn him.

On 30 May 1555 Cardmaker was taken by the sheriffs of London to Smithfield, along with John Warne, an uneducated upholsterer who had refused to recant unless he could be shown a passage in the Bible requiring him to do so. Warne said his prayers, was chained to the stake and had wood and reeds piled around him, ready to be set alight. Cardmaker, however, was embroiled in a long

Above: *The entrance to Smithfield market today*

However, to everyone's surprise, the prisoner was kept alive for another five months while the authorities made every effort to convert him. A succession of visitors streamed into his cell to engage in theological argument: bishops, laymen, former friends, and even two Spanish friars (later Roman Catholic archbishops in Spain). With threats and cajoling they sought to undermine his resolve and wear him down psychologically. Perhaps only Thomas Cranmer in Oxford was also treated this way. While Cranmer's faith was shaken, Bradford remained resolute. On one occasion the two friars stormed out in protest at his stubborn determination. Meanwhile Bradford's ministry in prison was as effective as it had been outside and he preached twice a day to his fellow inmates. When he saw condemned criminals on their way to execution, he would remark, 'But for the grace of God, there goes John Bradford.'

While Bradford remained alive, rumours circulated that he might be pardoned and released. The uncertainty continued for several months until the authorities finally ran out of patience. Then the end came swiftly. On Sunday 30 June 1555, the gaoler's wife ran up, anxious and out of breath: 'O master Bradford', she exclaimed, 'I come to bring bad news.' 'What is it?' he asked. 'Tomorrow you must be burned, and your chain is now being bought, and soon you must go to the Newgate.' At this the prisoner took off his cap, looked up to heaven and declared, 'I thank God for it. I have expected this for a long time and therefore it does not come to me suddenly, but as something waited for every day and hour. The Lord make me worthy of it!' He went back to his cell and spent the rest of the

Above: A memorial to the Smithfield martyrs, erected in 1870, on the wall of St Bartholomew's Hospital

evening praying with his friends, before they left in tears. It was nearly midnight when Bradford was transferred from the Poultry Compter to the Newgate, the authorities hoping that the streets would be empty—but there was a large crowd alongside Cheapside, weeping and praying for him as he passed by.

A young man was also to be martyred with Bradford: John Leaf, a nineteen-year-old tallow-chandler's apprentice. Leaf was illiterate, unable either to read or write, yet he resisted the arguments with which he was assailed by Bishop Bonner. When Bonner tried to persuade him to recant, the young man replied,

'My Lord, you call my opinion heresy, but it is the true light of the word of God.' In prison, two papers were placed in front of him. One was a full recantation, while the other was a copy of the statements he had made at his trial. When the first was read, Leaf refused to affix his mark. When the second was read, he seized a pin, thrust it into his hand and let the blood drip down as his signature.

It was rumoured that the martyrs would be burned at four o'clock in the morning, when everyone was still asleep, so Smithfield was crowded with people from an early hour. In fact the execution party did not arrive until nine o'clock. Nothing was left to chance. The guard was stronger than usual, with armed men on all sides. Bradford and Leaf were dragged to Smithfield on two hurdles, tied face downwards. When they arrived at the spot, they fell on the ground in prayer, but the sheriff insisted the proceedings be finished quickly because the crowd was so great. Bradford took up a bundle of reeds and kissed it. Then he kissed the stake, took off his outer clothing and was chained. The martyr held up his hands and cried, 'O England, England! Repent of your sins, repent of your sins. Beware of idolatry. Beware of false antichrists. Watch out that they do not deceive you.' He was silenced by the sheriff with a threat that his hands would

Above: Archdeacon Philpot prays at the stake, from Foxe's Book of Martyrs

be tied if he did not shut up. Bradford appealed for the onlookers to pray for him and encouraged young Leaf: 'Be of good comfort, brother, for we shall have a merry supper with the Lord tonight.' As Bradford embraced the reeds the last words the crowd could hear were 'Hard is the way and narrow is the gate that leads to eternal salvation, and only a few find it' (Matthew 7:14).

The courageous archdeacon

John Philpot was a knight's son and the Archdeacon of Winchester. Many times before, he had clashed with his pro-Catholic bishop, Stephen Gardiner. During the Convocation of October 1553, shortly after Mary came to the throne, Philpot was one of the few who spoke up for a Protestant understanding of the sacraments. He was shouted down and denounced, reportedly with the phrase 'You have the word, but we

have the sword.' Philpot was immediately arrested and sent to the King's Bench prison (near the Marshalsea in Southwark). There he engaged in heated disputes with radical Anabaptists, who were also sentenced to death for denying the divinity of Christ. He even spat in the face of one and wrote a pamphlet justifying his action.

The authorities did their best to persuade Philpot to recant, without success. He was examined more than a dozen times by various bishops between October and December 1555. Seeing that the prisoner would not be moved, Bonner eventually condemned him to death and pronounced him a 'heretic'. To this Philpot replied, 'I thank God that I am a heretic outside your cursed church: I am not a heretic before God. But God bless you and give you grace to repent of your wickedness. And let everyone beware of your bloody church.' As he was led away through the streets to the Newgate, he called out to the gathered crowd: 'Good people, blessed be God for this day.' His last nights in prison were ones of cruel treatment, being chained and abused.

At supper on Tuesday, 17 December 1555, a messenger came from the sheriffs of London telling Philpot to get ready because he would die the next day. The prisoner answered, 'I am ready. God grant me strength and a joyful resurrection.' He went to his cell and prayed earnestly, thanking the Lord for counting him worthy to suffer for the truth. The following morning, about eight o'clock, the sheriffs arrived to carry him to the place of execution. On reaching

Above: A single wall is all that remains of the Marshalsea, the second most important prison in England after the Tower of London. Bishop Bonner, a keen persecutor of Protestants under Mary Tudor, was eventually to die here himself in 1569

Smithfield, Philpot knelt down and proclaimed, 'I will pay my vows in you, O Smithfield!' He then kissed the stake and declared, 'Shall I disdain to suffer at this stake, seeing my Redeemer did not refuse to suffer a most vile death upon the cross for me?' The martyr recited Psalms 106, 107 and 108, gave away money to the guards, was bound to the stake and committed to the flames.

The secret congregations

And so the fires continued to rage unabated at Smithfield over the next few years. Protestants were hunted down and burned in small groups. In 1556, seven were martyred together in January, six in April and three in May. Another ten were burned during 1557. Before Mary Tudor's reign was over, the fires of Smithfield had claimed forty-three lives—more than any other place in England.

A number of those who died were members of secret congregations which met in or near London to pray and to read the English Bible. One such congregation was led by John Rough, a Scottish Protestant. Although it frequently changed its meeting place to avoid discovery, it was infiltrated by a government spy who sent reports back to the authorities. In December 1557 constables swooped on the congregation in the Saracen's Head Inn at Islington. Rough was arrested and soon burned. A deacon of the congregation,

Left: The Tudor courtyard of Fulham Palace, home of the Bishops of London, where Bonner interrogated suspected Protestants. Some he sent to the stake, others he personally flogged in his orchard

Cuthbert Symson, had been entrusted with the dangerous task of keeping a list of members and at Bishop Bonner's request he was taken to the Tower and stretched on the rack in an attempt to persuade him to divulge the names. Symson refused to buckle under torture and was burned at Smithfield in March 1558.

The following May another illegal congregation was discovered meeting in a field near Islington using the English liturgies of Edward VI. Some managed to escape, but twenty-two were arrested and thrown into Newgate prison. Bonner condemned thirteen to be burned—seven at Smithfield on 27 June and six the next day at Brentford (west of London). The armed guard in charge of the Smithfield executions issued a proclamation forbidding any spectator, under pain of imprisonment, to touch or speak to the martyrs. Nevertheless the onlookers pressed around and embraced them. Thomas Bentham (later Bishop of Lichfield under Queen Elizabeth) had recently returned from exile on the continent to pastor another secret congregation in London. He was in the crowd and shouted out: 'We know that they are the people of God and therefore we cannot but wish them well and say, God strengthen them! Almighty God, for Christ's sake strengthen them.' Others replied, 'Amen, Amen!' One of the seven in the fire, Roger Holland (a merchant tailor), embraced the stake and the reeds and prayed aloud: 'Lord, I humbly thank you that you have called me from death to the light of your heavenly word, and now to the fellowship of your saints, that I may sing, "Holy, holy, holy, Lord God of hosts!" And Lord, into your hands I commit my spirit. Lord, bless your people and save them from idolatry.' These were the last recorded words spoken at Smithfield during Queen Mary's reign of terror.

LONDON

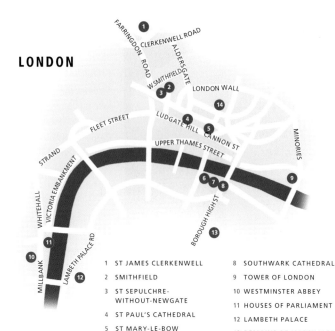

1 ST JAMES CLERKENWELL
2 SMITHFIELD
3 ST SEPULCHRE-
    WITHOUT-NEWGATE
4 ST PAUL'S CATHEDRAL
5 ST MARY-LE-BOW
6 CLINK PRISON
7 RUINS OF BISHOP OF
    WINCHESTER'S PALACE

8 SOUTHWARK CATHEDRAL
9 TOWER OF LONDON
10 WESTMINSTER ABBEY
11 HOUSES OF PARLIAMENT
12 LAMBETH PALACE
13 REMAINS OF MARSHALSEA
14 THE GUILDHALL

TRAVEL INFORMATION

Clink Prison Museum

Clink Prison Museum,
1 Clink Street, London, SE1
www.clink.co.uk
☎ 020 7378 1558

The Clink was the
Bishop of Winchester's
private prison, dating from
the 12th century; many
martyrs were sent here by
Stephen Gardiner. It
burned down during the
Gordon Riots of 1780. The
museum occupies a
Victorian warehouse on
the original site.

Fulham Palace

Fulham Palace, Bishop's
Avenue, London, SW6
☎ 020 7736 3233
Nearest tube station:
Putney Bridge.

Fulham Palace was the
residence of the
Bishop of London for over
twelve hundred years,
from 704 to 1973. At its
centre is a Tudor courtyard
and Great Hall, from the
time of Bishops Ridley and
Bonner. The Palace was
once enclosed by the
longest moat in England
and still has thirteen of its

original thirty-six acres of
land. The gardens, open to
the public, became
famous in the 17th
century when Bishop
Henry Compton imported
rare plant species to
Europe for the first time.
The Palace itself is usually
closed, though there are
guided tours by
arrangement. There is also
a small museum.

St Sepulchre-without-Newgate

St Sepulchre-without-
Newgate, Giltspur Street,
London, EC1

www.st-sepulchre.org.uk
☎ 020 7248 3826

St Sepulchre's is the largest parish church in the City of London. John Rogers was rector here from 1550. The tower and outer walls were built around 1450, but the church was gutted by the Great Fire of London. It was subsequently rebuilt by Sir Christopher Wren in 1670.

West Smithfield

West Smithfield, London, EC1

Smithfield, London's ancient meat market, was the scene of many executions, including those of religious radicals and political agitators (such as Sir William

Above: *Smithfield Martyrs' Memorial Church, since demolished*

St James Clerkenwell

'Braveheart' Wallace). Nearby is St Bartholomew the Great, London's oldest parish church, founded as an Augustinian priory in 1123 by Raherne, a monk and one of Henry I's courtiers. Raherne also founded the neighbouring hospital ('Barts'), London's oldest hospital.

St James Clerkenwell

St James Church, Clerkenwell Close, London, EC1
www.jc-church.org
☎ 020 7251 1190

The present church building dates from the 1790s and contains a large memorial plaque to the Smithfield martyrs. There was once a Martyrs' Memorial Church nearer Smithfield, opened in 1871, but this was pulled down after World War Two.

Southwark Cathedral

Southwark Cathedral, London Bridge, London, SE1
www.southwark.anglican.org/cathedral
☎ 020 7367 6700

For many centuries Southwark was part of Winchester diocese. St Swithin, Bishop of Winchester, is believed to have set up a college of priests in about AD 860 on this site next to the River Thames. In 1106 a new church, St Mary Overie ('over the river') was founded by two knights, with the help of Bishop William Giffard. His successor, Bishop Henry of Blois, built his episcopal palace nearby, which was occupied by the Bishop of Winchester until 1626. At the Reformation, the priory of St Mary Overie was surrendered to Henry VIII in 1539 and became St Saviour's parish church. In 1905 Southwark became a new diocese and St Saviour's was chosen as the cathedral. A statue of John Rogers forms part of the reredos.

③ The pastor of Hadleigh

The prosperous town of Hadleigh in Suffolk was one of the first places in England where Reformation teaching took root. But under Mary Tudor, the local rector—Dr Rowland Taylor—was burned at the stake, sending shock waves through the region

Rowland Taylor was born in Northumberland and studied law at Cambridge, where he came in contact with the leading reformers. Archbishop Cranmer chose him as one of his chaplains and as a close adviser on the reform of ecclesiastical law. In 1544 he was appointed by the archbishop to the important benefice of Hadleigh. Taylor was not a great theologian or scholar, and has left behind no academic treatises. He was, however, an energetic pastor and preacher. He was a large man, with a massive physique and a long white beard, known for his big heart and his care for the poor. He taught the Christian message with clarity and warmth, and reformed the parish according to Protestant principles. For example, the rich church furnishings, such as silver crosses, expensive chalices and candlesticks, altar cloths and vestments, were sold off and the money given to the needy.

When Mary came to the throne, Taylor was one of the first preachers to be rounded up. A warrant was issued for his arrest

Above and facing page: Hadleigh parish church. The Deanery Tower nearby (part of Rowland Taylor's rectory) was built in 1495 by a former rector, Archdeacon Pykenham, as the gateway to a great house that was never completed

on 25 July 1553, less than a week after the new queen was proclaimed. Taylor was imprisoned for three months, but surprisingly was pardoned and allowed to return to Hadleigh. This brief skirmish with the authorities was a foretaste of the battle to come.

Above: Rowland Taylor preaching—from a window in Hadleigh church

Resisting the invaders

In March 1554 two local men, Foster and Clerk, stirred up renewed persecution. They hired a Roman Catholic priest, John Averth (vicar of nearby Aldham) to come to Hadleigh parish church and perform the Latin mass. Taylor was at home at the time, studying his Bible. When he heard the church bells ringing, he went to investigate, but found the main church doors shut and barred. He entered through a side door and there discovered the tonsured priest, in vestments, about to begin the mass sacrifice. Around the altar were men with drawn swords, in case anyone should resist them.

Immediately Taylor challenged the intruder: 'You devil! Who made you so bold to enter this church of Christ, to profane and defile it with this abominable idolatry?' Foster responded, 'You traitor! What are you doing here, to obstruct the queen's proceedings?' 'I am no traitor', replied Taylor, 'but I am the shepherd that my Lord Christ has appointed to feed his flock, so I have good authority to be here. And I command you, you popish wolf, in the name of God, to go away and not dare to poison Christ's flock with such popish idolatry.'

The heated argument continued. Foster accused Taylor of being a heretic and of violent resistance. The reformer retorted, 'I resist only with God's word against your popish idolatries, which are against God's word, the queen's honour, and tend to the utter subversion of this realm of England.' At that Foster and his armed men threw Dr Taylor out of his church. His wife, who had followed close behind, was thrown out also and the doors locked. A crowd loyal to their rector gathered outside, some of whom hurled stones through the windows at the mass priest.

Foster and Clerk wrote immediately to Bishop Gardiner to complain of Taylor's actions. Knowing that he faced imprisonment and possible death, his friends urged him to flee. Yet Taylor considered it a 'glorious calling' to suffer for the gospel. He asked, 'What Christian would not gladly die against the Pope and his adherents? I know that the papacy is the kingdom of antichrist, altogether full of lies, altogether full of falsehood. All their doctrine is nothing but idolatry, superstition, errors, hypocrisy and lies.' 'Remember the Good Shepherd Christ', he explained, 'who not only fed his flock but also died for his flock. Him I must follow, and with God's grace, will do.'

Condemned

Taylor was sent to the King's Bench prison in London, where other leading reformers such as John Bradford, John Philpot and Robert Ferrar were also held. First he was deprived of his benefice for being married, so Mrs Taylor and her children were evicted from Hadleigh rectory. Then, in January 1555, he was put on trial at St Mary Overie in Southwark. In front of the court, the defendant publicly rejected the doctrine of transubstantiation as 'most wicked, idolatry, blasphemy and heresy'. Gardiner tried to persuade him back into the Roman Catholic Church, but he told the bishop to 'repent for bringing the realm of Christ to antichrist, from light to darkness, from verity to vanity.'

Taylor was condemned to be

Above: Rowland Taylor stands trial—from a window in Hadleigh church

burned to death for heresy. As he was taken back to gaol, he proclaimed to a crowd which had gathered: 'God be praised, good people. I have come away from them undefiled and will confirm the truth with my blood.' He later wrote to a friend: 'God be praised, since my condemnation I was never afraid to die: God's will be done. ... God be praised, even from the bottom of my heart, I am immovably settled upon the rock, not doubting that my dear God will perform and finish the work that he has begun in me and others.'

'Welcome the cross of Christ'—Laurence Saunders at Coventry

The second martyr of Mary Tudor's reign, burned the day before Rowland Taylor, was Laurence Saunders, minister of All Hallows Church, Bread Street in London. In October 1553, shortly after the queen's arrival in the capital, Saunders had preached a provocative sermon on the words of the Apostle Paul: 'I betrothed you to one husband, to present you as a pure virgin to Christ. But I am afraid that as the serpent deceived Eve by his cunning, your thoughts will be led astray from a sincere and pure devotion to Christ' (2 Corinthians 11:2-3). Everyone in the congregation knew to whom the preacher was referring, and that very day he was charged with treason, sedition and heresy. Bishop Gardiner interrogated him and cried, 'Carry away this frenzy-fool to prison.' When the burnings began, Saunders was taken to Coventry for execution and declared, 'I am the most unfit man ever appointed to this high office. But my gracious God and dear Father is able to make me strong enough.' He spent his last hours exhorting his fellow prisoners in Coventry gaol to turn to Christ.

On 8 February 1555, Saunders was led to a quarry known as the Hollows, in Cheylesmore Park, outside the city walls. He walked to the stake bare-foot, clothed only in an old gown and shirt. Several times on the journey he fell with his face to the ground in prayer. It was at the Hollows that nine Lollards had been burned to death between 1512 and 1522, for crimes such as teaching their children English versions of the Lord's Prayer and the Ten Commandments. Saunders was martyred on the same spot. The officer in charge of the execution proclaimed that Saunders deserved death because he had marred the queen's realm with his false doctrine. Yet he promised the prisoner that he would receive a royal pardon and escape the fire, even now, if he revoked his Protestant beliefs. Saunders answered, 'It is not I, nor my fellow-preachers of God's truth, who have hurt the queen's realm—but it is you yourself, and those like you, who have resisted God's holy word. It is you who mar the queen's realm. I hold no heresies, but the doctrine of God, the blessed gospel of Christ—that I hold, that I believe, that I have taught, and that I will never revoke.' The officer cried, 'Away with him', and the martyr was taken to be chained to the stake. Saunders fell on the ground one last time to pray. Then he embraced the stake and kissed it, saying, 'Welcome the cross of Christ, welcome everlasting life.'

Pictured: *The memorial to Lawrence Saunders and the Coventry martyrs, erected in 1910*

Above: Laurence Saunders is chained to the stake, from Foxe's Book of Martyrs

On 5 February, the prison guards allowed Taylor's wife and young son to visit him and eat supper together for the last time. In tears they prayed, and Taylor gave to his wife as a parting gift his precious copy of the reformed *Book of Common Prayer*, which he had used daily during captivity. At two o'clock in the morning, under cover of darkness, the prisoner was taken from his cell to begin the final journey back to Hadleigh. His wife had been watching from a distance, with two of their daughters, longing for another glimpse of their loved one. Taylor was briefly allowed to kiss them and bless them, and even some of the sheriff's men wept at the sight.

Home at last

For four days Rowland Taylor and his execution party travelled from London to Suffolk, passing through Brentwood, Chelmsford and Lavenham. On the journey, Taylor was forced to wear a hood over his head, with holes only for his eyes and mouth, lest passers-by recognise him and attempt a rescue. His final night was spent locked in the cellar of the Guildhall of Corpus Christi at Lavenham, only nine miles (fourteen kilometres) from Hadleigh. There he was offered the queen's pardon if he would return to the Roman Catholic Church. He was even promised a bishopric for converting.

On 9 February the prisoner and his guards set out on the last stage of their journey. When Hadleigh finally came into view, Taylor climbed from his horse and began dancing about. The sheriff was puzzled and asked if the pastor was feeling alright. 'God be praised, never better', replied Taylor, 'for now I know I am almost home. Two more stiles to go over and I am at my Father's house.'

The martyrs of East Anglia

Rowland Taylor was only the first of thirty-two Christians martyred in East Anglia under Mary Tudor. In the months that followed February 1555, twelve were burned for their faith at Bury St Edmunds, eight at Norwich, five at Ipswich, and others in smaller towns and villages around Suffolk and Norfolk.

Amongst those who suffered was Robert Samuel, vicar of East Bergholt, near Ipswich. The authorities raided his house in the middle of the night, drove out his wife whom he had refused to banish, and carried the preacher to prison. Samuel was tortured, being forced to stand chained to a post with only his toes on the ground and fed just two or three mouthfuls of bread a day. He was condemned as a heretic and burned in August 1555 at the Cornhill, in the centre of Ipswich. Another, martyred on the same spot, was Alice Driver, aged about thirty, whose ears were cut off for comparing Queen Mary to Jezebel. Her last recorded words at the stake, as an iron chain was fastened around her neck, displayed her courage: 'Oh, here is a good neckerchief. Blessed be God for it.'

In the 'Lollard's Pit' at Norwich, Simon Miller and Elizabeth Cooper were burned together in July 1557. Miller had stood outside a church and publicly declared his devotion to the communion service of the *Book of Common Prayer*. Elizabeth Cooper had entered a church while the mass was being celebrated and denounced the proceedings. In the fire she was terrified by the flames, but Miller managed to put an arm

Above: The martyrs' memorial at Christchurch Park, Ipswich

around her and encourage her that they would soon share 'a joyful and sweet supper' with the Lord in heaven. After witnessing this martyrdom, Cicely Ormes called out in a loud voice that she too held the same religious views. So she was burned at the same stake two months later.

As they entered the outskirts of the town, the first to greet them was a poor parishioner with five children to whom Taylor had ministered in the past. He prayed that God would help the rector and was sharply rebuked by the sheriff, but this was a token of things to come. On the streets of Hadleigh there was a popular

Left: Lavenham Guildhall, where Rowland Taylor spent his last night

outpouring of sympathy and grief. The roads were crowded on both sides with men and women, many weeping and praying out loud for their pastor. 'Oh good Lord! there goes our good shepherd, who has so faithfully taught us, so fatherly cared for us and so godly governed us.' 'O merciful God! What shall we poor scattered lambs do? What shall come of this most wicked world?' 'Good Lord strengthen and comfort him.' The sheriff and his men tried to keep the people quiet, but with no success.

En route to the stake, they passed the Hadleigh almshouses where Taylor had for years ministered to the poor and elderly inhabitants. These old men and women now stood at their doorways to see their pastor one last time. Taylor had been given money in prison by benevolent visitors, and what remained he distributed at the almshouses. An old blind couple who lived at the twelfth and last almshouse, were unable to come to their door, so the martyr placed his last coins in a glove and threw it through their window before riding on.

At last the party arrived at the place of execution on Aldham Common, a field just outside Hadleigh. Taylor got off his horse, tore the hood from his head and proclaimed, 'God be thanked, I am at home.' His attempts to address the crowd were prevented by one of the guards thrusting a staff in his mouth. He proceeded to give away his clothing, beginning with his boots and coat, until he stood there just in his shirt. The martyr did manage to utter one bold statement to the onlookers: 'Good people! I have taught you nothing but God's holy word, and those lessons that I have taken out of God's blessed book the holy Bible, and I have come here today to seal it with my blood.' At that the guards struck him hard on the head.

Not permitted to speak further, Taylor knelt down and prayed. A poor woman from the crowd ran forward and prayed with him— despite the guards' attempts to drag her away and their threats to trample her under their horses. Taylor went to the stake and kissed it. He was bound to it with chains and stood there with hands folded, eyes towards heaven, continually praying. The sheriff commanded a local butcher to set up the wood and reeds, but he refused, despite the threat of prison. Eventually four men were conscripted to start the fire. One threw a bundle of reeds at Taylor's face, causing blood to run down his cheek. As his executioners worked around him, the martyr recited Psalm 51 in English, and was again struck on the mouth and told to speak only Latin. When the fire was kindled, Taylor held up his hands and called upon God: 'Merciful Father of heaven, for Jesus Christ my Saviour's sake, receive my soul into your hands.' He stood patiently in the fire, until he was struck on the head with an axe and his skull split open.

A Protestant ministry continues

When Rowland Taylor was forced to leave Hadleigh in March 1554, he left the parish in the care of an assistant minister, Richard Yeoman, an elderly man in his seventies. But Taylor's successor as rector, John Nowell, threw out Yeoman and brought in a Roman Catholic curate instead. For a time Yeoman travelled from place to place, encouraging the Protestants he met and selling little packets of laces and pins to earn a living. Eventually he returned to his wife and children at Hadleigh, living in a secret room in the Guildhall, near the parish church. There he stayed for more than a year, spending his days in prayer, Bible study and the carding of wool for his wife to spin. She meanwhile was forced to beg for food to feed the family.

Above: Hadleigh's medieval Guildhall. It was here that Richard Yeoman lived in hiding before being sent to the stake in July 1558

Above: The martyrs' memorial at Bury St Edmund's, near the Cathedral

When Nowell heard of Yeoman's whereabouts, he raided the Guildhall in the middle of the night, breaking down five doors to reach the preacher. Yeoman was dragged from his bed and thrown in the stocks, alongside John Dale, a local weaver. Dale was being punished because he had described the rector and his curate as 'miserable and blind guides' who were ignorant of God's truth. At Nowell's insistence, Yeoman and Dale were transferred to prison at Bury St Edmunds, where they were harshly treated. Dale died in prison, aged forty-six, and Yeoman was moved again to Norwich. There he was put on trial and interrogated about his marriage and his views on transubstantiation. Required to submit to the Pope, Yeoman replied, 'I defy him and all his detestable abominations.' He was condemned and burned at the stake in the 'Lollard's Pit' on 10 July 1558.

In spite of these burnings, Reformation teaching was not totally extinguished from Hadleigh. After Yeoman was driven away, a young man called John Alcock used to go to the parish church every day to say the English litany and read a chapter from the English Bible. He was thrown in the stocks by the rector because he refused to doff his cap when a religious procession passed by. Nowell accused Alcock of being 'a heretic and a traitor', and personally ensured he was taken to London for trial and imprisonment. After a year in Newgate gaol the young Protestant died. His body was thrown out and buried in a dunghill.

After Queen Mary's death, Protestant ministry returned to the town of Hadleigh. Nowell was replaced as rector in 1560 by Thomas Spenser, who had been in exile on the continent and a member of John Knox's congregation at Geneva. Spenser was a Puritan and re-established the preaching of the Christian gospel for which Taylor had given his life.

HADLEIGH

A 1071
TO IPSWICH

TO SUDBURY
A 1071

RIVER BRETT

ANGEL STREET
GEORGE STREET

B 1070

KEY TO PLACES

1 MARTYRS' MEMORIAL
2 ROW CHAPEL AND
  ALMSHOUSES
3 ST MARY'S CHURCH
4 DEANERY TOWER
5 GUILDHALL

Lavenham Church

Lavenham Guildhall of Corpus Christi

Lavenham Guildhall,
Market Place, Lavenham
☎ 01787 247646
www.nationaltrust.org.uk

Built about 1530, this impressive timber-framed Tudor building dominates Lavenham Market Place. It is now owned by the National Trust.

TRAVEL INFORMATION

Lavenham

In the early 16th century Lavenham was one of the wealthiest towns in England dominated, like Hadleigh, by the woollen cloth industry. Many historic houses survive from that period, as well as a magnificent church, one of Suffolk's famous 'wool churches'. William Gurnall, the Puritan author of *The Christian in Complete Armour*, was minister here between 1644 and 1679.

St Mary's Church, Hadleigh

The present church, built in the 15th century, is part of the old medieval heart of Hadleigh. It stands on the site of a 9th century Saxon church, the burial place of Guthrum, Danish King of East Anglia and a convert to Christianity. In the south chapel are two memorials to Rowland Taylor—a brass plaque from the 1590s and a stained-glass window from the 1880s.

Near to the church are the Guildhall and the Deanery Tower, both closed to the public. It was in the rectory that Hugh James Rose convened a small clerical conference in July 1833 which was a catalyst for the Oxford Movement.

Above: A large number of Tudor houses survive in Lavenham

parishioners. They were replaced by new almshouses further from the street in 1887. The chapel is still in use and a key is kept in a nearby almshouse.

Row Chapel, Hadleigh

Row Chapel, George Street, Hadleigh

This 15th century chapel was originally a wayside chapel for travellers. Under the will of Archdeacon Pykenham, twelve almshouses were built alongside, for twenty-four poor

The martyrs' memorial, Hadleigh

Next to the Hadleigh by-pass (A1071), opposite Lady Lane

Standing in a farmer's field on the site of Taylor's martyrdom is a pyramidal monument from 1819. It includes an

interesting poem in praise of Taylor's courage. At the foot of this memorial is a much older stone, which has marked the spot since the end of the 16th century.

This Monument was erected.
1819
by private Subscription
The Reverend Richard Yeoman. Curate to Dr Taylor after a series of the most cruel persecution which he endured with exemplary patience and fortitude suffered martyrdom at Norwich 10th of July 1558.

Restored by the Parishioners, May.
1882.

④ The radical bishops

As Mary Tudor's campaign of persecution began to gather pace, it soon took the lives of two Protestant bishops—John Hooper and Robert Ferrar. These men were kindred spirits. They were known as the two most radical reformers in the episcopate and were martyred only seven weeks apart

John Hooper began his career as a Cistercian monk at Cleeve Abbey in Somerset. He was converted to the principles of the Reformation through studying the writings of the continental reformers, in particular Ulrich Zwingli and Henry Bullinger. He began to teach these ideas passionately, but was forced to flee from England in the early 1540s when Henry VIII promoted an anti-Protestant reaction within church and state. Exiled to mainland Europe, Hooper married a Flemish wife and settled in Zurich, where he wrote theological treatises and developed a close friendship with Bullinger who was a mentor of many English Protestants.

In May 1549, two years after the accession to the throne of Edward VI, Hooper returned home. He was an able preacher and quickly rose to prominence, winning the support of Archbishop Cranmer and the new king. His radical Protestant views meant he was known as 'the Zwingli of England'. In April 1550 Hooper was offered the

Above: *The cloisters at Gloucester Cathedral*

Facing page: *View of Gloucester Cathedral*

bishopric of Gloucester, but refused it because he would have to swear an oath by the saints and wear medieval vestments, which he described as superstitious and anti-Christian. This led to a clash with the other leading reformers, known as 'the vestiarian controversy'. Many failed attempts to persuade him to

Above: Hooper was an able preacher. His sermons on Jonah were delivered before King Edward VI during Lent 1550

change his views, led to Hooper finally being sent into solitary confinement in the Fleet prison for refusing to obey the Act of Uniformity. After almost three weeks locked up, he submitted to wearing vestments and was consecrated bishop in the chapel of Lambeth Palace in March 1551. Hooper set about reforming his diocese, and was shocked to discover the levels of ignorance amongst his clergy. Of three hundred and eleven examined, one hundred and seventy-one could not name the Ten Commandments, ten could not recite the Lord's Prayer, and twenty-seven did not know by whom the Lord's Prayer was first taught.

Like Hooper, Robert Ferrar began his career as a monk, a member of the Augustinian priory of St Oswald at Nostell, near Pontefract in Yorkshire. However, he too showed early signs of Reformation sympathies and was arrested in Oxford in the late 1520s for possessing banned Lutheran literature. He became an itinerant Bible teacher in the north-east of England and won the favour of Thomas Cromwell, the chief adviser on church affairs to Henry VIII. In 1548, under Edward VI, Ferrar was appointed Bishop of St David's in south Wales and began to reform the diocese, working to improve the morality of his clergy and their standards of preaching. His episcopate was sadly marred by bitter legal battles with his cathedral chapter (some of them keen Protestants), who tried to prise him out of his post and have him imprisoned.

Deposed and condemned

When the persecution began under Queen Mary in 1553, Hooper and Ferrar were among the first reformers summoned before the authorities in London. Hooper's friends advised him to run for his life, but he replied, 'Once I did flee and take to my feet, but now because I am called to this place and vocation I will stay, to live and die with my sheep.' Hooper was thrown into the Fleet prison and Ferrar into the King's Bench prison, where they remained for many months. In March 1554 they were both deposed from their bishoprics—as were four other bishops—for being married. Hooper was treated with particular cruelty by the warden of the Fleet. He was often kept in solitary confinement in a filthy cell, with a bed of straw covered by a rotting blanket. His letters were confiscated and money sent by friends was not allowed to get through. Hooper became seriously ill, but when he called for help the warden refused to open the cell door and ordered his guards not to respond, since it would be 'good riddance' if the bishop died in prison.

At the end of January 1555, Hooper was taken to St Mary Overie in Southwark where he was put on trial before Bishop Gardiner. Found guilty of heresy, he was condemned to death and transferred to the Newgate prison near Smithfield. On Monday 4 February, he and John Rogers were both degraded by Bishop Bonner and expected to be burned together as the first two martyrs under Mary. Rogers was taken straight to Smithfield, but Hooper was surprised to be told he would die at Gloucester amongst his former flock. At this he praised God and, ever practical, immediately sent for his boots, spurs and cloak that he might be ready for the journey.

At four o'clock the following morning, the bishop was taken from his cell, searched, and handed over to six royal guards—his armed escort for the three day

Above: Hooper's final lodgings, according to tradition. They are some of the oldest surviving timber-framed buildings in Gloucester and now house the Folk Museum

ride to Gloucester. Lest he be recognised, he was forced to wear a hood under his hat, with holes only for his eyes and mouth. Nevertheless, news of Hooper's return went ahead of them and when the party reached the outskirts of Gloucester on Thursday evening they were met by a large crowd. The people were so numerous and clearly sympathetic to Hooper, that his guards feared a rescue attempt. In fright, one rode ahead into the city to call the mayor and sheriffs of Gloucester, who came and ordered the crowd to disperse. The prisoner was lodged in the house of Robert Ingram, opposite St Nicholas' Church, where he spent his last full day on earth.

Degradation

Before being burned at the stake, ordained ministers first had to suffer the humiliating ceremony of 'degradation'. The medieval equivalent of 'unfrocking'. This ritual reduced bishops and clergymen back into laymen. Bishops Hooper, Ferrar, Ridley and (probably) Latimer were only degraded from the priesthood, not from the episcopate, because the Roman Catholic authorities did not recognise them as bishops. In Hooper's case this was because he had been consecrated using the Reformed ordinal of 1550 which was deemed invalid.

The process of degradation followed a set pattern. First the condemned man was dressed in the traditional vestments of his office, and then stripped of them one by one. When these priestly garments were forced upon Bishop Ferrar before his martyrdom, he boldly spoke against them as 'rags and relics of Rome'. Those being degraded had their fingers, thumbs and the crowns of their heads scraped with a rough knife, to remove the oil of anointing. It is said that when Archbishop Cranmer was degraded, Bishop Bonner deliberately cut his fingers while scraping them. A wafer representing the host was put in the condemned clergyman's hands and then removed, to show that he was no longer worthy to hold it. The bishop conducting this ceremony then symbolically struck him on the breast with his crosier-staff and declared that he was deprived of his right to preach the gospel. Some, such as Rowland Taylor, also had their hair cut off.

Unexpected visitors

Hooper spent most of his last hours in private prayer. However, his devotions were interrupted throughout the day by unexpected visitors.

First an old friend, Sir Anthony Kingston, came to see him. Kingston had benefited from the bishop's ministry and in particular the urgent call to repent from sexual immorality, but now he had been appointed as one of the commissioners to supervise the burning. As soon as he saw Hooper, Kingston burst into tears and pleaded with him to recant. 'Remember', he said, 'that life is sweet and death is bitter'. 'That is true', replied the martyr, 'but the life to come is more sweet and the death to come is more bitter.' Hooper explained that he would rather suffer the torment of fire than deny the truth of God's word.

That afternoon, a blind boy, Thomas Drowry, persuaded the guards to let him visit the bishop. The lad had recently been imprisoned in Gloucester for his faith and, with tears in his eyes,

Hooper encouraged him: 'Ah, poor boy! God has taken away your outward sight, but he has given you another sight much more precious, for he has endued your soul with the eye of knowledge and faith.' Drowry himself was to be burned in Gloucester in May 1556. Next to visit was a Roman Catholic who expressed sorrow for Hooper. The bishop retorted that the man should keep his pity for himself because of his 'wicked' beliefs and that death for Christ's sake was not to be lamented but welcomed.

Last of all, as the evening drew near, the mayor, aldermen, and sheriffs of Gloucester came to greet Hooper. He thanked them for their kindness, asked that the execution be quick, and protested that he died a true and obedient subject of the queen but was willing to give up his life 'rather than consent to the wicked papistical religion of the Bishop of Rome.' The bishop was formally handed over into the custody of the sheriffs, who wanted to move him to the city gaol. However, the royal guards interceded, insisting that Hooper was a well-behaved prisoner, so he was allowed to remain at Ingram's house.

When these interviews were over, Hooper ate supper and retired to bed very early, at five o'clock. He slept soundly during the first part of the night and then rose to pray through the small hours, insisting that he be left alone until the morning.

Above: The tall spire of St Nicholas' Church, opposite the building in which Hooper was lodged the night before his death in February 1555

A lamb to the slaughter

Hooper's execution was set for Saturday 9 February 1555—the same day that Rowland Taylor was burned to death at Hadleigh. At nine o'clock in the morning the sheriffs arrived at the bishop's lodgings to escort him to his death. With them was an armed posse of guards, carrying swords and axes, but when the prisoner saw their many weapons, he protested, 'I am no traitor. You do not need to make such a commotion. If you had allowed me, I would have gone to the stake alone and troubled none of you.'

It was market day and almost seven thousand people crowded

the streets, trying to get a sight of the martyr or to hear his last words. Hooper was strictly forbidden to speak to them, but he explained to those nearby that he was being executed because he had preached true doctrine from the word of God and would not now declare it heresy. He was led out between the two sheriffs to the place of execution on a small green just outside the cathedral precincts, known as 'St Mary's Knapp'. The journey was short, but Hooper walked slowly, resting on his staff. The pain of sciatica, caused by harsh treatment in prison, forced him occasionally to stop. The crowd along the route wept for their bishop, but he smiled at those he recognised, looking more cheerful, some said, than ever he had before. At the guards' insistence Hooper remained silent, led, observed John Foxe, 'like a lamb to the slaughter' (Isaiah 53:7).

St Mary's Knapp was packed with spectators. Some had climbed up trees to get a better view; others leant out of the windows of local houses. The dean and chapter, with other ecclesiastical dignitaries, had the best vantage point of all, from the windows of St Mary's Gate, the main entrance into the cathedral precincts. At the stake, Hooper knelt and prayed earnestly for half an hour. His prayers were interrupted by the arrival of a box, laid before him on a stool, containing a pardon from the queen if he should recant. On seeing the box, the bishop cried, 'If you love my soul, take it away! If you love my soul, take it away!'

When his prayers were finished, Hooper prepared for the fire. He took off his gown, which was borrowed from Robert Ingram, asking that it be returned to its owner. The sheriffs insisted he strip further, down to his shirt,

Right:
St Mary de Lode Church, near the site of Hooper's execution

Above: *Hooper going to his martyrdom, from a painting by Michael William Sharp (1776-1840)*

since they wanted the rest of his clothing. Hooper was then bound to the stake by an iron hoop around his waist. Further irons were brought for his neck and legs, but he refused them, promising that he would not try to run from the fire. As bundles of wood and reeds were placed around him, he took some in his arms, embraced them and kissed them. He freely forgave the man in charge of making the fire and encouraged him to do his task well. As the pyre was lit, the reformer began to pray, 'O Jesus, Son of David, have mercy on me and receive my soul!'

Unfortunately the fire was badly made. As a result, Hooper's suffering was protracted and he had to endure excruciating pain. Most of the wood was green and failed to burn. It was also a cold

and windy morning, so at first the flames were blown away from the martyr and merely licked him. A second fire had to be constructed, with drier wood. This burned Hooper's legs, but did not reach the top half of his body, except for singeing his hair and scorching his skin. When the flames died down, Hooper wiped his eyes and cried out, 'For God's love, good people, let me have more fire.'

At last a third fire was kindled, fiercer and more effective than the other two. Again the martyr prayed with a loud voice: 'Lord Jesus, have mercy on me! Lord Jesus, have mercy on me! Lord Jesus, receive my spirit!' These were the last words he was heard to utter, yet still he remained alive. His mouth was black, his tongue swollen, his lips shrunk to the gums as he continued to call out to

God. His legs were burned off and when he beat his breast one of his arms fell off into the fire. His other hand was melted on to the iron hoop around his waist. After forty-five minutes of extreme agony, the martyr's strength was finally gone. He bowed forwards and died.

Ferrar follows

Meanwhile, back in London, Bishop Ferrar was still in prison. Instead of being condemned at St Mary Overie alongside the other reformers, like Rogers, Taylor and Hooper, it was decided he should stand trial in his former diocese. Therefore, on 14 February 1555, Ferrar was sent down to Carmarthen in south Wales, the main town in the diocese of St David. In the place where he had once exercised great authority, he was now kept as a common prisoner. He was examined in the parish church of St Peter's, Carmarthen—the very building where he had once presided over his own consistory court. In Ferrar's old chair sat the new bishop, Henry Morgan, who had already set about depriving Protestant clergy in the diocese and replacing them with his own appointees. As the prisoner stood in front of the court he recognised a number of faces—men who had worked alongside him in previous years.

There were a series of hearings in late February and early March, during which Ferrar was questioned about transubstantiation, the celibacy of the clergy, and justification. He was pressed to recant his Protestant 'errors' and to affirm Roman Catholic orthodoxy—but he refused. He rejected the

Above: Hooper at the stake, from Foxe's Book of Martyrs
Above, right: The charred stump, reputedly, of the stake at which Hooper was burned. It was discovered by workmen in 1826 extending the churchyard of St Mary de Lode, and is now in the Gloucester Folk Museum

Above, left: St Mary's Gate, built in the 13th century, the main entrance to the medieval abbey precincts. From the first storey windows, the dean and chapter watched Hooper's burning

Above, right: The memorial to Hooper on the site of his martyrdom, erected in 1862. Ironically, the bishop is shown wearing the ecclesiastical vestments which he so detested. This picture is taken through St Mary's Gate

authority of Morgan to be his judge, but the new bishop angrily condemned him to death. Ferrar was degraded and then handed over to the sheriff of Carmarthenshire, Griffith Leyson, for his final days in prison. Two weeks before Easter, on 30 March 1555, the martyr was burned in the market place, not far from the gates of Carmarthen Castle. As he was bound to the stake, he tried to address the crowd but was forbidden. His last minutes were ones of excruciating pain. Death was prolonged, perhaps because those who built the fire used slow-burning peat. Nevertheless this new martyr stood patiently at the stake, until he was dashed on the head with a staff and fell into the fire.

On the same day that Ferrar died at Carmarthen, a second Welsh martyr, Rawlins White, was burned at Cardiff. White was an elderly and illiterate fisherman, but he had sent his young son to school to learn to read. Every evening after supper, his son read to him from the English Bible and White was soon able to recite long passages by heart. He began to preach locally, exhorting and encouraging others to turn to Christ. The Bishop of Llandaff condemned him to death, and he was executed in Cardiff High Street, in front of a great crowd.

The continental reformers

There was a close relationship between the reformers in England and the reformers on the European mainland. They shared theological ideas and personal encouragements, often interacting through public debate and private correspondence. The four continental reformers with the biggest impact in England were Martin Luther, Ulrich Zwingli, Henry Bullinger and John Calvin.

Martin Luther was the trailblazer of the Reformation in Germany. He launched his attack upon the theology and practice of the Roman Catholic Church in 1517 by nailing ninety-five 'theses' to the door of the Castle Church in Wittenberg. This passionate appeal for the reform of the church soon reverberated around Europe. In 1521 Luther was summoned to the Diet of Worms and told to retract his writings, but refused to do so, claiming his conscience was 'captive to the word of God'. His famous declaration, 'Here I stand, I cannot do otherwise', became a rallying cry of the Reformation. In

England, King Henry VIII argued against Luther's view of the sacraments and so was given the title *Fidei Defensor* ('Defender of the Faith') by the Pope. However, Luther's writings were soon in circulation and were being debated by Cranmer, Latimer, Tyndale and others at the White Horse Inn in Cambridge. 'Lutheran literature' became a byword for any early Protestant books—such as those read by Ferrar in Oxford in the 1520s. Luther's colleague, Philip Melanchthon, was the main author of the Augsburg Confession (1530), which directly influenced the Church of England's Thirty-Nine Articles.

In Switzerland, the cause of reform was first pioneered in Zurich by Ulrich Zwingli. When Zwingli was killed on the battlefield in 1531, he was succeeded as chief minister by Henry Bullinger, who remained there until his own death in 1575. During Mary Tudor's reign, Bullinger hosted a number of prominent exiles from England and continued a voluminous correspondence with them after they returned home (known as *The Zurich Letters*). He remained a

theological advisor to many English clergy and even to Queen Elizabeth herself. Bullinger's sermons on Christian doctrine, *The Decades,* became a standard textbook in Elizabethan England.

Elsewhere in Switzerland, in Geneva, the leader of the Reformation was John Calvin. He became chief minister there in 1536 having fled persecution in France and in turn welcomed persecuted Protestants from England in the 1550s. Calvin published many Bible commentaries, two of which were dedicated to Edward VI, and a great work of systematic theology, *The Institutes of the Christian Religion*. The definitive 1559 edition of *The Institutes* was translated into English in 1561 by Thomas Norton, son-in-law of Archbishop Cranmer. Another significant publication to emerge from Geneva was the *Geneva Bible* (1560), an English translation with extensive marginal notes from a Calvinist perspective. It was dedicated to Queen Elizabeth and, although never authorized in England, became hugely popular in Puritan circles.

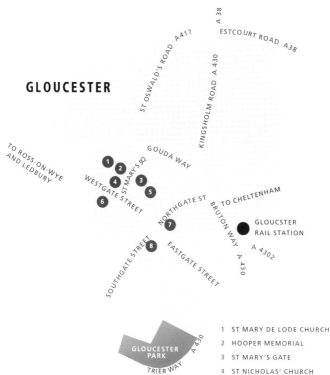

GLOUCESTER

1 ST MARY DE LODE CHURCH
2 HOOPER MEMORIAL
3 ST MARY'S GATE
4 ST NICHOLAS' CHURCH
5 GLOUCESTER CATHEDRAL
6 GLOUCESTER FOLK MUSEUM
7 NEW INN
8 OLD BELL INN

TRAVEL INFORMATION

Gloucester Cathedral

Gloucester Cathedral,
Gloucester
www.gloucestercathedral.
org.uk
☎ 01452 528095

St Peter's abbey was founded in Gloucester by King Osric in 679. The abbey church was totally rebuilt after the Norman Conquest, with the construction of the great tower as late as the 1450s. At the Reformation under Henry VIII, the

Pictured: *Window at Gloucester Cathedral, showing three Christians tortured with fire—St John (boiled in a cauldron), Bishop Hooper (burned at the stake) and St Lawrence (roasted on a gridiron)*

Above: The London Sergeant's mace. It bears the arms of Philip and Mary on the head and those of the City of London at the end of the handle. It was probably carried by the royal guards bringing Hooper to Gloucester and is the only such brass mace in existence

The New Inn was originally built as a pilgrim's inn, to house visitors to the shrine of King Edward II in St Peter's Abbey. It was rebuilt in 1450 and is one of the best surviving examples of a medieval galleried inn. It was here that Lady Jane Grey heard the news that she was to succeed Edward VI, and she was proclaimed queen from the inn's gallery on 10 July 1553.

abbey was dissolved in 1540 and its property confiscated. The church was rededicated to the Holy and Indivisible Trinity and became the cathedral of the new diocese of Gloucester. In the north aisle is a stained-glass window depicting Hooper's burning.

Gloucester Folk Museum

Gloucester Folk Museum, 99-103 Westgate Street, Gloucester
www.livinggloucester.
co.uk
☎ 01452 396467

Gloucester Folk Museum is housed in splendid Tudor and Jacobean buildings, dating from the 16th and 17th centuries. It was

here, according to tradition, that Hooper spent his last two nights. The museum contains a number of Hooper artefacts, including the remains of the stake and the mace carried by his royal guards.

The New Inn, Gloucester

The New Inn, 16 Northgate Street, Gloucester
www.newinnglos.com
☎ 01452 522177

The Old Bell Inn, Gloucester

The Old Bell Inn, Southgate Street, Gloucester
☎ 01452 332993

Another of Gloucester's famous hostelries, the Bell Inn was the birthplace of George Whitefield in 1714. He was baptised nearby at St Mary de Crypt Church and preached his first sermon there in 1736. The south chapel of the church is dedicated to Robert Raikes, founder of the Sunday School movement, who also lived in Southgate Street. There is a statue of Raikes in Gloucester Park.

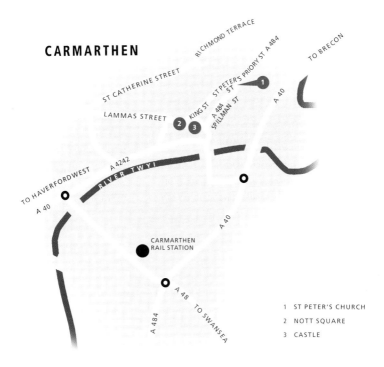

CARMARTHEN

1 ST PETER'S CHURCH
2 NOTT SQUARE
3 CASTLE

Carmarthen Castle

Carmarthen Castle stands on a rocky outcrop overlooking the River Twyi. It was first built by the Normans, but sacked by Llywelyn the Great in 1215 and again by Owain Glyndwr in 1405. It was captured during the Wars of the Roses in 1469 and largely demolished during the English Civil War in the 1640s. The remains of the castle became the county prison in 1789 and now contain council offices.

St Peter's, Carmarthen

St Peter's Church, St Peter's Street, Carmarthen
www.stpeterscarmarthen.org

St Peter's is the parish church of Carmarthen and one of the largest churches in the diocese of St David's. The building dates from the 11th century and contains many interesting memorials. Walter Devereux, the first Earl of Essex and Queen Elizabeth I's favourite, is buried here. The consistory court was used for administering ecclesiastical law and contains a memorial to Bishop Ferrar (pictured).

Above: Brentwood's Swan Inn today, on a different site to that in Hunter's time

'I understand your mind well enough', said the sumner. 'You are one of those who hates the queen's laws. You must turn over a new leaf, or else you and a great many more heretics will burn for it, I promise you.'

'God give me grace that I may believe his word and confess his name, whatever the consequences', came the reply.

'Confess his name!' exclaimed Atwell. 'No, no, you will go to the devil.'

The official went to find someone else who could persuade Hunter of his errors. Sitting in a nearby inn was Thomas Wood, vicar of South Weald and chaplain of Brentwood, who agreed to accompany Atwell in dealing with the young Protestant. Back in the chapel they found him still reading.

'Who gave you permission to read the Bible', asked the vicar, 'and to expound it?'

Hunter again explained that he was not expounding the Scriptures but only reading them for his own benefit.

'Why meddle with them at all?' questioned Wood. 'It does not suit you, nor those like you, to meddle with the Scriptures.'

'I will read the Scriptures (God willing) while I live,' insisted Hunter, 'and you ought not to discourage any one from doing so.'

'How dare you tell me what I should do? I see you are a heretic!'

'I am no heretic for speaking the truth.'

And so the argument continued. Mainly they debated transubstantiation and the correct interpretation of passages such as chapter six of John's Gospel. At one point Hunter challenged the vicar: 'I wish that you and I were even now tied fast to a stake, to test which of us would stand strongest in our faith. I think I know who would recant soonest.' At that, Wood and Atwell departed breathing threats.

A Brentwood bonfire

Knowing that he was now in danger for his life, young Hunter fled from Brentwood into the countryside. The local magistrate, Sir Anthony Browne, immediately ordered his arrest. Browne intimidated Hunter's father, threatening to throw the old man into prison if he did not produce his son. After two or three days the young Protestant returned to Brentwood of his own volition, rather than place his parents in jeopardy. He was put in the stocks before being sent down to London to be interrogated by Bishop Bonner. At first the bishop was gentle, promising to send him home if only he would recant. Yet when the teenager stood firm, he was threatened with death. For nine months he was left languishing in prison.

When the burnings of Protestants began at the start of 1555, Hunter was swiftly despatched. On 9 February he was condemned by Bonner in the consistory court at St Paul's Cathedral, along with five others. Even after the sentence had been pronounced, the bishop tried to win him over. Hunter was promised £40 to set up his own business (a significant sum in the 1550s) or employment in Bonner's own household at Fulham Palace, if only he would admit his errors. The prisoner responded, 'I thank you for your great offers, my Lord, but if you cannot persuade me from the Scriptures, I cannot turn from God for love of the world. I count all worldly things as loss and dung compared to the love of Christ.'

'If you die in those opinions you are condemned for ever', the bishop warned.

'God judges justly and justifies those whom man condemns unjustly', came the confident reply.

THE ELM TREE.

Above: The original Martyr's Tree, near which Hunter was burned

Below: The tree that stands on the site today

THIS OAK WAS PLANTED
TO MARK THE ACCESSION OF
H.M.KING GEORGE VI IN 1936,
AND TO REPLACE THE ANCIENT ELM
NEAR WHICH WILLIAM HUNTER
WAS BURNT TO DEATH FOR HIS BELIEFS,
MARCH 26th, 1555.
THE DECAYED STUMP OF THE OLD TREE
WAS REMOVED IN 1952.

The following month, the six prisoners condemned by Bonner were taken from their cells in the Newgate and sent to various towns and villages around Essex to be burned—as a warning to the local populace. Hunter was taken back to Brentwood where he was kept under guard in the Swan Inn for three nights. There his parents visited him for the last time. His mother exhorted her son to continue in his Protestant faith, prayed for God to strengthen him, and declared that she was delighted to have a child who was willing to lose his life for Christ's name. Hunter in turn encouraged her: 'For the little pain I shall suffer, which shall soon end, Christ has promised me, mother, a crown of joy. May you not be glad of that?' Other friends came to the Swan to bid the martyr farewell and he admonished them to turn from 'the abomination of Popish superstition and idolatry.'

The night before his execution Hunter dreamed vividly about being burned and the details of his dream were to be accurately fulfilled the next day. On the morning of Tuesday, 26 March

Above: Hunter is encouraged by his parents, from a Victorian engraving

1555, men armed with swords and bows arrived at the Swan to convey him to his death. The young man walked confidently through the gathered crowd carrying his precious English Psalter. The stake was set up on the outskirts of town near a great elm tree, known from that day as 'The Martyr's Elm'. When they arrived at the spot Hunter knelt down on a bundle of reeds to recite Psalm 51, interrupted by accusations that he was using a heretical translation.

At that moment the sheriff produced an official document and announced, 'Here is a letter from the queen. If you will recant you shall live, if not you shall be burned.'

'No, I will not recant, God willing', answered the martyr and stood with his back against the stake to be chained to it. 'Good people, pray for me', he called, 'and despatch me quickly. Pray for me while you see me alive.'

'No', declared Sir Anthony Browne, who had come to witness the scene. 'I will no more pray for you than I will pray for a dog.'

'Mr Browne', said Hunter, 'now you have what you sought for and I pray it will not be laid to your account on the last day.

Above: Brentwood Grammar School, founded in 1557 by Sir Anthony Browne, who came to regret his part in the burning of William Hunter

However, I forgive you.'

'I ask no forgiveness from you', retorted Browne.

'Well', replied the Protestant, 'if God does not forgive you, I shall require my blood at your hands.'

It was an overcast day and Hunter suddenly cried out, 'Son of God, shine upon me.' Immediately, to the astonishment of the crowd, the sun broke through a dark cloud and shone full in his face, forcing him to turn his head away. He then took up a bundle of reeds and embraced it. When the fire was about to be lit, a Roman Catholic priest made one last attempt to persuade him to recant. 'Away, you false prophet', shouted Hunter. 'Beware of them, good people, and come away from their abominations, in case you share in their plagues.'

'As you burn here', replied the priest, 'so you shall burn in hell.'

'You lie, you false prophet', insisted Hunter. 'Away, you false prophet, away.'

In defiance of the authorities, someone in the crowd prayed for God to have mercy on the young man's soul, to which many responded 'Amen, Amen'. As the fire was kindled Hunter threw his Psalter to his brother, Robert, who shouted back: 'William, think about the holy passion of Christ and do not be afraid of death.'

'I am not afraid', called the martyr as the flames rose around him. Lifting his hands to heaven, he cried, 'Lord, Lord, Lord, receive my spirit', before being smothered by the smoke. Once Hunter had died, Magistrate

Browne dashed straight from Brentwood to the village of Horndon-on-the-Hill to witness the burning of Thomas Higbed, the second Essex martyr. Thomas Causton suffered that same day at Rayleigh. Within a fortnight there were further burnings at Braintree, Maldon, Colchester, Rochford and Coggeshall as the persecution continued to spread throughout the county.

It is said that Sir Anthony Browne soon repented of his part in Hunter's death. Two years later he founded Brentwood Grammar School near the spot where the young man had been killed, apparently in atonement for his cruelty. To this day the Brentwood School song contains the lines

> They bound a lad by a green
> elm tree
> And they burnt him there for
> folk to see.
> And in shame, for his brothers
> and play-mates all,
> They built then a school with a
> new red wall.

The red-brick wall of the school still stands. After many centuries the great elm tree died and was replaced by an oak, still known locally as 'The Martyr's Tree'.

Ten Colchester candles

Colchester, the ancient county town of Essex, saw more martyrdoms under Mary Tudor than any other place in England, except Smithfield and Canterbury. The first to be burned was John Lawrence, a converted friar, on 29 March 1555. He had been so brutally treated in prison, bound with heavy irons upon his legs, that he was no longer able to walk. They carried him to the fire in a chair and he was burned sitting down. At the stake he was surrounded by a group of small children who chanted, 'Lord, strengthen your servant and keep your promise! Lord, strengthen your servant and keep your promise!' Lawrence was followed over the next three years by twenty-two other martyrs in Colchester.

Right: Edmund Tyrrell burns Rose Allen's hand, as she fetches water for her sick mother. From Foxe's Book of Martyrs

Above: Memorial to William Hunter in Brentwood, erected in 1861. It declares, 'Christian reader, learn from his example to value the privilege of an open Bible and be careful to maintain it'

The town's bloodiest day was 2 August 1557, when ten Protestants were executed within ten hours. Amongst them were three members of one family from the village of Great Bentley—William and Alice Munt, with Alice's daughter, Rose Allen, aged twenty. They had previously been arrested for their Protestant sympathies and released, but persisted in their refusal to attend mass at the parish church, preferring to meet in secret for prayer and Bible reading. The local vicar reported the family to the authorities and in March 1557, at two o'clock one morning, their house was surrounded by armed guards. The guards commanded that the door be opened and they dragged the Munts from their bed. They also found another couple, John and Margaret Thurston, hiding in the house.

Edmund Tyrrell, the officer in charge of the arrest, was one of Bishop Bonner's henchmen and zealous in hunting down Protestants. He began an argument with Rose, accusing her of being a heretic, and he threatened, 'I perceive you will burn, gossip, with the others.' (At that time the word 'gossip' meant 'old woman' and was used by Tyrell as an insult).

'I hope in Christ's mercies, if he calls me to it, he will enable me to bear it', she replied.

Tyrrell turned to his associates and taunted, 'This gossip will burn, don't you think?' At that he took her by the wrist and held her hand over a candle flame until the flesh burned away as far as the bone.

'You young whore, won't you cry?' he cursed, and thrust her away with profane abuse. Rose remained composed, insisting that Tyrrell had more reason to weep than she did. 'If you think it good', she proclaimed defiantly, 'begin at my feet and burn my head also. He who set you to work will pay you your wages one day, I promise you!'

Under examination later in prison, Rose was equally fearless. She proclaimed that Roman Catholic doctrine 'stank in the face of God' and that her interrogators would have the reward of antichrist if they did not repent. When asked if she would submit to the authority of the see of Rome, she mocked, 'that sea is for crows, kites, owls and ravens like you to swim in. By the grace of God I will not swim in that sea while I live or have anything to do with it.'

The Munts, the Thurstons and Rose Allen were taken to Colchester Castle—the main prison for the county of Essex— soon to be joined by John Johnson. Meanwhile there were another six Protestants locked up at the Moot Hall—the main prison for the town of Colchester. John Thurston died in prison and his wife's execution was delayed, but the others were burned on the same day, 2 August. Before seven o'clock that morning, the six from the Moot Hall were taken to a plot of ground just outside the city wall, where they knelt down to pray. The youngest, Elizabeth Folkes, aged twenty, was kissed by her mother who had come to

The antichrist and the whore of Babylon

Many of the Protestant martyrs denounced the Pope as the 'antichrist' and the Roman Catholic Church as the 'whore of Babylon'. This was a popular form of polemic at the time of the Reformation.

According to the New Testament, the antichrist opposes Jesus Christ, teaching what is false and deceiving the church (1 John 2:18-23, 4:1-3).

He is often identified with the 'man of sin' (2 Thessalonians 2:1-12), who claims to be from God but is actually in league with Satan. He is also identified with the beasts of the Book of Revelation, who persecute Christ's followers and promote idolatry (Revelation 13). Closely allied to the beasts is 'Babylon the Great', the mother of prostitutes, drunk with the blood of the saints (Revelation 17).

At different stages in Christian history, the antichrist has been interpreted as a reference to various historical figures—such as Nero, Mohammed, Napoleon or Hitler. In the 16th century, the Protestant reformers understood the Church of Rome to be teaching falsehood, promoting idolatry and persecuting Christ's true followers. Therefore they naturally identified the Pope as 'antichrist himself' and Rome as the 'whore of Babylon' or 'the seat of Satan'.

Above: Colchester Castle

watch, and exhorted to be strong in the Lord. Elizabeth took off her petticoat and threw it away, proclaiming, 'Farewell all the world, farewell faith, farewell hope.' She then embraced the stake saying, 'Welcome love!' One of the officers nailing the chains around the prisoners missed his aim and struck Elizabeth on the shoulder with his hammer. She raised her eyes to heaven and prayed with a smile, before admonishing the crowd. When all six were firmly bound, they clapped their hands for joy as the flames rose around them. There were several thousand onlookers who encouraged the martyrs with cries of 'The Lord strengthen them! The Lord comfort them! The Lord pour his mercies upon them!' That same afternoon, the four condemned prisoners in Colchester Castle were burned to death in the castle bailey. They called on the name of God and earnestly pleaded with the crowd to flee idolatry. Eye-witnesses remarked on the joyful triumph of their last moments.

The queen's largest blaze

The small Essex village of Stratford-le-Bow, on the main road from London to Colchester, witnessed a number of martyrdoms in 1555 and 1556. Amongst those burned to death on the large village green were Hugh Laverock, an elderly and disabled painter who walked with a crutch, and John Apprice, who was blind. They were betrayed to the authorities by a neighbour in May 1556 and hauled before Bishop Bonner. The bishop examined them in his consistory court in St Paul's Cathedral, particularly on the subject of transubstantiation, and urged them to recant. Laverock had objected to the elevation of the host during the mass and he declared, 'I will stand by my answers. I cannot find in the Scriptures that the priests should lift over their heads a cake of bread.' Bonner met with similar determination from blind Apprice: 'Your doctrine is so agreeable with the world and entwined with it, that it cannot be agreeable with the Scriptures of God. You are not of the Catholic Church, for you make laws to kill men and make the queen your hangman.' The two Protestants were quickly despatched. They were carried from the Newgate in a cart to Stratford-le-Bow to be burned. As they were being chained to the stake, Laverock threw away his crutch and encouraged his fellow martyr: 'Be of good comfort, my brother, for the Bishop of London is our good physician. He will heal us both soon, you of your blindness and me of my lameness!' And so they died, praising God.

The following month Stratford-le-Bow witnessed a mass execution. Thirteen Protestants—eleven men and two women—were burned together in the largest fire ever seen in Mary Tudor's reign. They were arrested in various parts of Essex and several were imprisoned in Colchester Castle, before being sent down to London for interrogation by Bonner. There they jointly subscribed to a written confession of faith, sternly rejecting the authority of the Roman Catholic Church as 'the church of antichrist, the congregation of the wicked, of which the Pope is head under the devil.' They likewise described the Latin mass as 'a profanation

Above: The old Moot Hall, the town prison for Colchester since Norman times, demolished in the 19th century

Right: Colchester's Town Hall today, which stands on the site of the old Moot Hall

Above, left: Memorial to the Colchester martyrs, erected in 1901, in the Town Hall

Above, right: Stratford martyrs' memorial, erected in 1878 in the churchyard of St John's Church

of the Lord's Supper ... a blasphemous idol.' For these bold views they were condemned and, on Saturday 27 June 1556, were transported shackled from the Newgate to Stratford. The sheriff in charge of the execution divided the prisoners into two groups and then attempted to undermine their faith by deception. He went to the first group and told them that the others had recanted, and that they would be saved if they did likewise. Yet the martyrs replied that their faith was built not on man but on Christ crucified and his word. The sheriff then went to the second group and lied to them that the

first group had recanted, only to be rebuffed with a similar response. The eleven men were tied to three stakes, surrounded by a ring of wood and reeds, piled high. The two women (one of them pregnant) were allowed to run free between the stakes. So they all perished in one fire, watched by a crowd of twenty thousand people.

The public revulsion at these constant executions had little impact on Bishop Bonner. He continued undaunted with his policy of persecution, sending more Protestants to the stake than any other bishop.

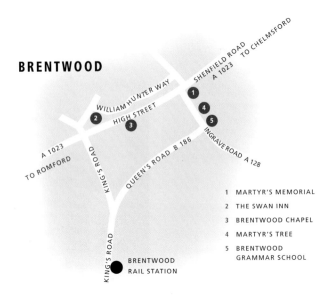

BRENTWOOD

1 MARTYR'S MEMORIAL
2 THE SWAN INN
3 BRENTWOOD CHAPEL
4 MARTYR'S TREE
5 BRENTWOOD GRAMMAR SCHOOL

TRAVEL INFORMATION

Colchester Castle Museum

Colchester Castle, High Street, Colchester
www.colchestermuseums.org.uk
☎ 01206 282939

The massive keep of Colchester Castle was built between 1076 and 1125 on the foundations of the Roman Temple of Claudius. It has been altered considerably over the centuries, the top part demolished in the 1690s. The surviving ruin was adapted in the 18th century by Charles Gray MP, for his own personal use. The castle is now a museum.

Colchester Town Hall

Colchester Town Hall, High Street, Colchester
☎ 01206 282222

There has been a town hall on this site for more than eight hundred years. The original Moot Hall was built in about 1160 and pulled down in 1844. The present Town Hall, opened in 1902, contains a memorial to the Colchester martyrs, but is closed to the public. Opposite the memorial stands a bust of Charles Spurgeon, who lived in Colchester and was converted there (see the Day One travel guide, *Travel with C. H. Spurgeon* by Clive Anderson).

St Peter's, Colchester

St Peter's Church, North Hill, Colchester
www.stpeterscol.org.uk

St Peter's is one of the few churches with its own entry in the Domesday Book of 1086. The present building has a fine Georgian interior and galleries which survive intact. There is a memorial to the Colchester martyrs, erected in 1843, near the Lord's Table (pictured).

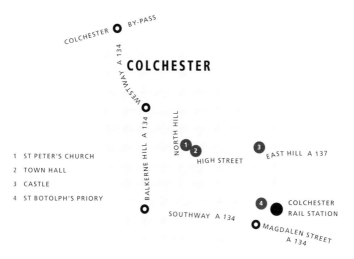

1 ST PETER'S CHURCH
2 TOWN HALL
3 CASTLE
4 ST BOTOLPH'S PRIORY

Above: *The red brick west tower of St Peter's, Colchester, erected in 1758*

Stratford-le-Bow

St John the Evangelist's Church, Stratford Broadway, London, E15
www.stjohnse15.freeserve.co.uk
☎ 020 8503 1913

Stratford-le-Bow was once a small village in Essex which has since grown into Greater London. St John's Church was built in 1834, to designs by Edward Blore, on Stratford Green where the Protestant martyrs were burned. The Stratford martyrs' memorial, erected in 1878, stands in the churchyard.

IN MEMORIAM
GEORGE MARSH MARTYR
BURNED AT CHESTER APRIL 24 1555

⑥ The martyr of the north

Under Mary Tudor the great majority of the martyred Protestants were killed in the south-east of England. Only one was burned to death north of the River Trent—George Marsh, the ploughman turned preacher

Georeorge Marsh was born about 1515, in the parish of Deane, near Bolton, in Lancashire. First he worked as a farmer, but when his young wife died, Marsh left their children in the care of his mother and went up to Cambridge to study theology. There he became familiar with the teaching of the leading reformers, and in May 1552 was ordained by Bishop Ridley. Marsh worked as curate to Laurence Saunders (the second martyr under Mary Tudor) in London and Leicestershire. He was also appointed by Edward VI as an itinerant 'preaching minister' for Lancashire, teaching the Christian message in Eccles, Bury and Bolton.

Above: Smithills Hall near Bolton

Facing page: Deane parish church, near Bolton. The cross in the foreground was erected in 1893 in memory of George Marsh

Run or stand?

When the persecution of Protestants began, Marsh planned to leave England for exile, perhaps in Denmark or Germany. In March 1554, just days before his departure, he returned home to Deane one last time to bid farewell to his family. However, the Earl of Derby—the Lord Lieutenant of Lancashire—had instructed any justice of the peace to arrest the preacher if his whereabouts became known. Eager to prove his anti-Protestant sympathies, Sir Robert Barton, a local magistrate, sent officers to find Marsh and ordered him to appear the next day at Smithills Hall, his manor house.

At first Marsh was undecided about whether to surrender or flee for his life. His mother and friends advised him to escape, but Marsh did not want people to think he was running away from his Christian beliefs. After a night of

The Green Chamber at Smithills Hall, where Marsh was examined, March 1554

The bloody footprint

There is a strange legend connected with George Marsh at Smithills Hall. It is said that he was so provoked by the taunts of his accusers, that when he descended the stairs from the Green Chamber he stamped his foot on the stone floor with such force that it bled. Marsh looked up to heaven and prayed that in that place there would be a permanent memorial to the wickedness and injustice of his enemies. At the bottom of the stairs there remains to this day an unusual mark on the flagstone, said to be his bloody footprint. Generations have tried to scrub it away, with no success. This legend, first recorded in 1787, was further embellished by the American novelist, Nathaniel Hawthorne, for his romance, *Septimius Felton* (1872).

earnest prayer and heart-searching, and an unexpected letter from a friend urging him to 'boldly confess the faith of Jesus Christ', he decided to submit to the summons. He was determined to 'bear such cross as it should please God to lay upon my shoulders.' Early the next morning he rose for prayer, saying the English Litany (as was his habit), and then spoke for the last time with family and friends. After a tearful departure from his mother and young children, Marsh walked the couple of miles across the hills of Bolton to Smithills Hall. There he was taken to an upper room, known as 'the Green Chamber', to be quizzed by Barton who was accompanied by his chaplain and officers. After much verbal abuse, Marsh was ordered to appear the next day before the Earl of Derby himself at Lathom House in West Lancashire.

'Blood-suckers' at Lathom House

Lathom House was a huge fortified mansion, crowned with towers; it was demolished a century later during the English Civil War. There Marsh faced Lord Derby and his council, which included a number of other Lancashire gentry and clergy. They examined the prisoner about his former ministry and his views on transubstantiation, asking him to write down answers to detailed theological questions. Marsh refused to comply, insisting that

Above: Lancaster Castle from the air

they were 'blood-suckers' who were trying to trap him and wanted him dead. After stern threats, Derby had him locked up in solitary confinement for two nights in a small, cold room where he was forced to sleep on the floor.

For the next fortnight, Marsh was constantly pressed to acknowledge that the Roman Catholic Church was the one true church. Both by the Earl and his council and in private conversation, he was quizzed about transubstantiation and auricular confession (the Roman Catholic practice of confessing sins to a priest) and urged to forsake his Protestant opinions. At one point, the vicar of Prescot discussed these topics with Marsh and reported to the council that his answers were sufficient for a beginner and someone still learning. Lord Derby was so delighted with this news that Marsh was given a bed and a fire, and was allowed to associate with the servants in the House. Yet the prisoner bitterly reproached himself for not confessing Christ more boldly. He prayed that God would strengthen him with his Holy Spirit and deliver him from his accusers' 'enticing words ... and deceitful vanity'. The next time he met with the vicar of Prescot he courageously asserted that the doctrine of the mass was offensive and unbiblical. Marsh was given Roman Catholic books to read and Roman Catholic articles to sign, but he refused to give ground. Although his family and his life were 'dear and sweet' to him, he insisted he would not

The geography of persecution

George Marsh was unique as the only Protestant burned to death in the north of England. Most martyrdoms under Queen Mary took place in the south-east, especially in London, Essex, East Anglia, Kent and Sussex. A handful of Protestants were executed in the midlands, but only three in Wales (all of whom were English) and only one in the south-west (Agnes Prest at Exeter).

This uneven geographical distribution was due to a number of factors. In part, it depended on the zeal with which the local bishop and his allies hunted down Reformation sympathizers. Several of the bishops in the south-east were notorious for the determination with which they tried to rid their dioceses of Protestants. Hottest amongst the persecutors were Bishop Bonner of London, Bishop Day of Chichester, Bishop Griffith of Rochester, Bishop Thornden of Dover and Bishop Hopton of Norwich.

The major factor, however, in the frequency of martyrdoms was the relative strength of Protestantism in the south-east. London and the surrounding counties were more cosmopolitan—centres of education and commerce, in close proximity to the European mainland. This part of the country was therefore often at the forefront of innovation and debate, and was more welcoming of radical ideas such as the Reformation. In contrast, the outlying regions of England and Wales were more theologically and culturally conservative. They resisted the erosion of their traditional way of life, which revolved around medieval Roman Catholicism. Indeed in some areas, such as Devon and Cornwall, there had been riots when the authorities in London ordered that the long-established Latin mass be replaced by the new English *Book of Common Prayer*. The Reformation made slow progress in many of these districts and they returned to Roman Catholicism without complaint when Mary Tudor came to the throne. It was in the south-east that religious radicalism was most vibrant and so it was also there that religious persecution was most severe.

Above: Lancaster Castle from the river

deny his faith in Christ under any circumstances. Marsh described himself as 'a sheep appointed to be slain' who would 'patiently suffer whatever cross it shall please my merciful Father to lay on me.' Faced with such resilience, Lord Derby sent the reformer to Lancaster Castle.

Praying and 'preaching' in prison

Marsh was kept in Lancaster Castle for nine months, probably in the Dungeon Tower (since demolished). Whilst there, he received many visitors. Some were friends or sympathisers, including the Mayor of Lancaster, who brought encouragement and practical gifts, such as money or food. They helped him smuggle out letters to his family and former parishioners. Other visitors, with good intentions, advised him to avoid death, but Marsh rebuked them with the words of Christ to Simon Peter: 'Get behind me, Satan'. Roman Catholic priests were also sent to argue with him, sometimes six at once, but as the preacher observed, 'priests are not always the greatest scholars or the most learned in God's law.' After their discussions about transubstantiation, the priests reportedly either ended up agreeing with Marsh or left with nothing to say.

Four times the prisoner was taken before the judges, with irons on his feet. It was claimed that he knew many other Protestants in Lancashire who were secretly spreading reformed opinions, and he was pressed, without success, to divulge their names. The judges also rebuked him for his habit of 'preaching' to people outside the prison walls. Twice every day Marsh and his cell-mate, Warburton, read together prayers from the English liturgy and chapters from the English Bible, but they did so at the top of their voices so that many others could hear. As a result people from the town gathered each night under Marsh's cell window to eavesdrop on this Protestant prayer meeting, much to the annoyance of the authorities.

In early 1555 Dr George Cotes, the newly enthroned bishop of Chester, visited Lancaster. He took Marsh's gaoler to task for allowing the 'heretic' the freedom to receive visitors and commanded that he be kept in less comfort with less food. Shortly afterwards Marsh was ordered to appear in person at Chester before the bishop himself.

A last chance to recant

In the hall of the bishop's palace in Chester, Cotes interrogated George Marsh about the doctrine of the mass. When the reformer failed to agree with his ecclesiastical superior, he was locked up in the Abbey Gateway, nearby. Here many clergy were sent to reinforce the bishop's arguments. They did all within their power to persuade Marsh to submit to the Church of Rome, but he would only describe it as a church 'of hypocrites and wicked worldlings'. Refusing to acknowledge the claims of the Pope, Marsh insisted that he trusted in Christ alone for his salvation.

When private persuasion proved useless, Marsh was taken to the Lady Chapel in Chester Cathedral for formal examination. The bishop sat in judgment, surrounded by church and civic dignitaries. Marsh was charged with having preached heresy and blasphemy in the parishes of Deane, Eccles, Bolton, Bury and elsewhere in the diocese. He was presented with a number of articles of belief and had to answer simply 'yes' or 'no' to each of them. No discussion was allowed and his replies were carefully recorded by the registrar

Above: *The Abbey Gateway in Chester, where George Marsh was imprisoned by Bishop Cotes*

Above: Chester Cathedral

before the prisoner was sent back to his cell.

Three weeks later Marsh was back in the Lady Chapel for sentencing, surrounded by armed guards. Again the bishop and his court were arrayed before him. The chancellor of the diocese, George Wenslow, began with an oration to the gathered crowd. He explained that the bishop was a good shepherd with his people's best interests at heart. The bishop, he said, was attempting to save and cure poor Marsh, a 'diseased sheep', and prevent him from infecting others in the flock. Marsh was reminded of his 'heretical' answers at the previous hearing and asked if he would stand by them. The martyr replied that he believed only those opinions which were publicly taught and legally established

Above: The Lady Chapel at Chester Cathedral, where George Marsh was condemned to death in 1555

under Edward VI, and in that 'pure religion' he would 'by God's grace, stand, live, and die.'

At this, the bishop pulled out of his coat pocket the sentence of condemnation and began to read. When he was almost halfway through, the chancellor interrupted, 'My lord, wait, wait, if you proceed any further it will be too late to recall it.' So the bishop waited. Priests and people called on Marsh to recant, whilst some knelt down to pray for him. He proclaimed that he loved Queen Mary as much as anyone and desired her mercy, but would not deny his Saviour Jesus Christ, for then he would lose everlasting mercy and win everlasting death.

The bishop replaced his spectacles and continued to read the sentence. After another five or six lines, the chancellor again interrupted with a smile and a show of mercy. 'My lord', he said, 'once again wait, for if that word is spoken, all is past, no relenting will then be possible.' The proceedings were now in danger of descending into a farce, but the bishop took off his spectacles and stopped. Once more the onlookers pleaded with Marsh to recant and save his life. 'I would like to live as much as you', asserted the martyr,

Above: Chester's Northgate today, a Georgian neo-classical arch from 1807

Top: Chester's heavily fortified medieval Northgate, in Marsh's time

Above: Gallows Hill today

Below: George Marsh's execution, from Foxe's Book of Martyrs

'but I will not deny my master Christ, lest he deny me before his Father in heaven.' The bishop continued to the end of his sentence, condemning Marsh to death. Afterwards he added, 'Now I will no more pray for you than I will for a dog.' The reformer, undaunted but still gracious, replied that he would nonetheless pray for the bishop.

'Not upon that condition'

George Marsh was handed over to the secular authorities and carried to his last prison, beneath Chester's Northgate. This grim underground dungeon, known as 'Dead Men's Room', was excavated from the rock thirty feet below ground level. The most infamous cell was 'Little Ease', measuring only four feet six

inches high and seventeen inches wide, into which unfortunate prisoners were squeezed. The only way air could enter the dungeon was through pipes from the street above, and here Marsh sat through long hours in the cold and dark. Sometimes at night friends

Above: Oak carving of Marsh's martyrdom, from the Lord's Table at Deane parish church

called down to him and threw him coins, which he needed to buy food and other necessities from the prison guards. The martyr invariably replied that he rejoiced to suffer for the gospel and was praying for 'grace not to faint, but patiently to bear his cross.'

On 24 April 1555 the two city sheriffs arrived at the Northgate with a motley crowd of armed barbers (the city police), carrying their rusty swords and poleaxes. Marsh was taken from the dungeon and to Gallows Hill, the site of public executions at Boughton just outside the city, overlooking the River Dee. He walked to his death with shackles on his feet, carrying his Bible and reading to himself. Some of the spectators offered the martyr money, so that he could pay a priest to say masses for his soul, but he told them to give it to the poor.

When they reached the stake, Marsh was shown the royal pardon, under the queen's seal, available for him if he would recant. He declared that he would gladly accept it, but could never do so upon that condition. Instead he began to preach to the people, explaining why he was to die and exhorting them to stick to Christ—until one of the sheriffs cut him short. Marsh knelt down to pray, discarded his outer clothing, and was chained to the stake. Wood and reeds were piled around him and, in a cruel twist, a barrel of pitch and tar was placed above his head, so that he was both burned and scalded to death. The fire was badly made and it was a windy day, so Marsh's agony was prolonged. His legs were slowly burned off and his body became black and swollen. The onlookers thought he was dead, when suddenly the martyr raised his arms and cried out one last time: 'Father of heaven, have mercy on me!'

The crowd was impressed by Marsh's patience in death, despite his extreme sufferings. They spoke of him as a godly Christian, which caused Bishop Cotes to preach a sermon in Chester Cathedral the next Sunday declaring that Marsh was a heretic, burned like a heretic and was now 'a firebrand in hell'. Meanwhile Marsh's friends gathered up his ashes and buried them in the cemetery of a small Leper Hospital near Gallows Hill.

1   SMITHILLS HALL
2   DEANE PARISH CHURCH

Deane Parish Church

Deane Parish Church, Junction Road, Bolton
www.deaneparish.info

Deane parish church is one of the oldest church buildings in Bolton, dating from 1452. The Lord's Table has a carving of Marsh's martyrdom. In the north aisle is the George Marsh memorial window, erected in 1897, which depicts Faith, Charity and Hope. There is also a fine Elizabethan pulpit, the oldest in Lancashire. In the churchyard, beside the main path, is the George Marsh memorial cross, erected in 1893. The church is usually closed, but visits can be arranged with the Rector of Deane,
☎ 01204 61819

Smithills Hall

Smithills Hall, Smithills Dean Road, Bolton
www.smithills.org
☎ 01204 332377

Smithills Hall is set in the two thousand acre Smithills Country Park. The medieval manor house includes a Great Hall (built about 1335) and oak-panelled Withdrawing Room (built about 1537).

CHESTER

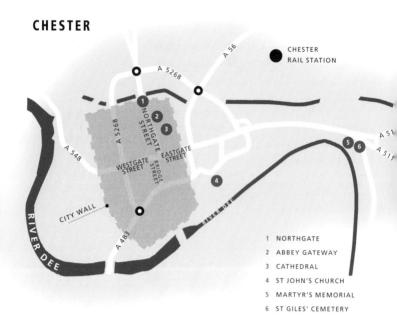

1 NORTHGATE
2 ABBEY GATEWAY
3 CATHEDRAL
4 ST JOHN'S CHURCH
5 MARTYR'S MEMORIAL
6 ST GILES' CEMETERY

Above: *The arms of Archbishop Cranmer, in Smithills Hall chapel*

The chapel contains a fine display of Tudor heraldic glass, including the arms of Archbishop Cranmer. The Hall is open to the public, but permission is needed to see the Green Chamber.

Lancaster Castle

Lancaster Castle, Castle Hill, Lancaster
www.lancastercastle.com
☎ 01524 64998

Lancaster Castle occupies an impressive hilltop site, overlooking the town. It is made up of an extensive group of historic buildings, including a Norman keep, 14th century Well Tower, and 15th century Gatehouse. Much of the castle is closed to the public, because it is still used as a Crown Court and prison. However, several parts are open, including the dungeons.

Chester Cathedral

Chester Cathedral, Chester
www.chestercathedral.com
☎ 01244 324756

Chester Cathedral was once a Benedictine

Abbey, founded in 1092. Most of the present building dates from the 13th to the 15th centuries. At the dissolution of the monasteries under Henry VIII, the abbey was closed in 1540 and became the cathedral of the newly-created diocese of Chester. The Lady Chapel, where George Marsh was condemned, is beyond the high altar.

Chester City Walls

Chester is the only city in Britain which retains the complete circuit of its defensive walls. First built when the Romans founded their fortress at Chester around AD 74, the walls have been repaired and restyled many times since. It takes between one and two hours to walk their full two mile (three kilometre) length, although they can be joined at many points.

St John's Church, Chester

St John the Baptist Church, Little St John's Street, Chester

One of Chester's ancient churches, St John's was begun by Peter, Bishop of Mercia, in the 11th century and used as his cathedral. Near the Lord's Table is a tablet in Marsh's memory, erected in the 1860s.

Above: The memorial to George Marsh on Gallows Hill, erected in 1898. In 1980 the name was added of a Roman Catholic priest, John Plessington, who in 1679 was hanged, drawn and quartered on Gallows Hill at the time of the 'Popish Plot' to assassinate King Charles II

Above: The remains of St Giles' Cemetery, Boughton—known as 'The Mount'—where Marsh's ashes were buried. The cemetery was once attached to the leper hospital of St Giles, founded in the 12th century and destroyed when Cromwell's army laid siege to Chester in 1643 during the English Civil War

Above: Memorial to George Marsh in St John's Church, Chester

Top: St Michael at the Northgate, to which the Bocardo was once attached

Above: The door of the cell in which the martyrs were imprisoned in the Bocardo

20 April, the three men were summoned to St Mary the Virgin Church, where they were pronounced heretics and excommunicated. The authorities claimed a resounding theological victory, but soon abandoned their plan to hold a similar disputation at Cambridge with Hooper, Ferrar, Taylor, Bradford and Philpot.

Having been condemned as heretics, the three reformers now anticipated death any day. They were separated and sent to three different prisons in Oxford to await execution: Cranmer back to the Bocardo, Ridley to the house of Alderman Edmund Irish, and Latimer to the house of one of the bailiffs. There they remained, to everyone's surprise, for the next sixteen months! When the burnings began in February 1555, all had expected the Oxford trio to die first.

The bishops' treatment in prison varied from month to month. Sometimes their keepers were gentle—they were well fed, permitted to exercise, and were allowed their books. At other times their keepers were harsh— they were forbidden visitors and their writing materials were confiscated. The reformers spent many of their last days writing letters of encouragement and spiritual counsel to friends and fellow prisoners. Ridley, in particular, wrote unceasingly, composing theological treatises and conducting a lengthy correspondence with John

people trying to speak at once. A noisy and partisan audience crowded into the building and proceeded to heckle the bishops. At the end of the week, on Friday

Pictured: *Entrance to the Divinity School in Oxford, from the Old Schools Quadrangle*

Bradford in the King's Bench prison in London. When his materials were removed, Ridley would make do with whatever scraps of paper he could find and sharpened the window lead to make pencils. The authorities had occasional success in discovering the reformers' letters, but a considerable number were smuggled out of prison undetected. As the persecution of Protestants intensified around the country, Ridley wrote to Cranmer at the Bocardo, outlining the stark choice which faced them all: 'Turn or Burn'.

'Play the man'

In the late summer of 1555, events in Oxford took a new turn. A papal delegation arrived, headed by Bishop Brooks of Gloucester, with instructions to ascertain whether Cranmer, Ridley and Latimer still held the same views on transubstantiation that they had expressed in the disputation of April 1554. First, on 12 September, Archbishop Cranmer was summoned to face the delegation at St Mary's Church. He made a point of taking his cap off to the two royal proctors on his left and right, but refused to acknowledge the bishops who formed the panel. He would be obedient to the crown, he explained, but totally rejected papal authority. The prisoner was examined and given eighty days to appear in person in Rome—an

The big three

For two decades Thomas Cranmer, Hugh Latimer and Nicholas Ridley worked as close allies—powerful advocates of the Protestant principles which they had learned while scholars together at Cambridge in the 1520s.

Cranmer's rise to the pinnacle of the Church of England was meteoric. He first came to the attention of Henry VIII in 1529 by defending the king's divorce from Catherine of Aragon—a fact never forgotten by Catherine's daughter, Mary Tudor. By 1533 Cranmer had been appointed as Archbishop of Canterbury, from which prestigious position he was able to encourage ecclesiastical reform. At first he had to proceed cautiously, but under Edward VI was given a free hand. Amongst Cranmer's many legacies to the Church of England were encouraging Henry VIII to

Cranmer

authorize the Bible in English, and the provision of reformed liturgies in the *Book of Common Prayer*.

Hugh Latimer was known as one of the greatest preachers of the Reformation in England. He was often invited to preach before Henry VIII, who made him a royal chaplain in 1534 and Bishop of Worcester in 1535. Four years later Latimer was forced to resign his bishopric as a result of a pro-Catholic reaction within the church. He was imprisoned, banned from visiting London, Oxford, Cambridge or Worcester, and ordered to stop preaching. Yet when Edward VI came to the throne, Latimer was able to return to a public preaching ministry with his customary vigour. He declined to reclaim his bishopric and lived instead with Cranmer at Lambeth Palace, assisting him in the

Ridley

implementation of various reforms.

Nicholas Ridley became one of Cranmer's chaplains in 1537, after identifying himself with the aims of the Reformation. He was soon appointed vicar of Herne in Kent and elected in 1540 as Master of Pembroke Hall, Cambridge. It was Ridley who persuaded Cranmer in about 1546 that the presence of Christ in the Lord's Supper is 'spiritual' rather than 'corporeal'. Ridley's influence increased considerably on the accession of Edward VI. He was consecrated as Bishop of Rochester in 1547 and promoted within three years to Bishop of London, where he became a figurehead of the Protestant cause.

Latimer

Pictured above:

The three Oxford martyrs, from the Martyrs' Memorial. Cranmer holds an English Bible which at his initiative was distributed in May 1541 throughout the parish churches of England

impossible request to fulfil. While the authorities waited for the Pope's formal verdict, Cranmer's life would be spared.

Two weeks later, on 30 September, Latimer and Ridley were summoned to the Divinity School for interrogation. Like Cranmer, Ridley pointedly refused to acknowledge the authority of the court. Having taken off his hat on entering the schools, he ostentatiously replaced it when the Pope's name was mentioned, and it had to be forcibly removed by the beadle. Under examination he admitted that he had once been a supporter of papal supremacy, but then again St Paul had once been a persecutor of Christ. The next day proceedings moved to St Mary's to hear the verdict and a large crowd packed the church. Almost everyone of note in the University and the city was there.

Above: *Detail from the Oxford martyrs' memorial. The open Bible and communion cup symbolise the truths on which the reformers staked their lives*

Top: *The Divinity School, with its elaborate fan-vaulted ceiling. The numerous bosses are carved with the initials or coats of arms of those who contributed to the cost*

Ridley was not allowed to read out the written defence he had prepared, but had been promised 'forty words' to explain why he rejected the Pope. That promise was now interpreted literally—as he began to speak, the audience counted out each of his forty words and he was silenced. Ridley refused to recant and so was condemned to death. Shortly afterwards Latimer was brought into the church and received the same judgment.

A fortnight passed before their execution. In the meantime a Spanish Dominican friar, Pedro de Soto, was sent to visit the prisoners but received a frosty reception. Seventy-year-old Latimer spent his last days quietly, in prayer and Bible reading. Ridley wrote many farewell letters, exhorting his friends to hold fast to the gospel, while denouncing Rome as 'the seat of Satan' and the 'whore of Babylon', and the Pope as 'antichrist himself'. When it came to their degradation by Bishop Brooks, Ridley was again obstructive and spoke constantly against the Pope, until he was threatened with being gagged. During his last evening at the Irishes' house they ate well—a shoulder of mutton, a pig, a plover, bread, cheese and pears. Ridley was in high spirits and spoke of his 'wedding' the next day. At this even Mrs Irish, who had at first been hostile to her prisoner, wept profusely. The martyr reassured her that although his breakfast might be 'sharp and painful', yet his supper would be 'pleasant and sweet'. George Shipside, Ridley's brother-in-law, offered to sit up with him during the night, but the bishop refused, declaring, 'I intend, God

Above: The church of St Mary the Virgin where Cranmer, Ridley and Latimer were condemned in 1555. Its 14th century decorated spire is the largest of the 'dreaming spires' of Oxford

Above: Balliol College, Oxford. Ridley and Latimer were burned in a ditch close by, followed five months later by Cranmer

willing, to go to bed and to sleep as quietly tonight as ever I did in my life.' Meanwhile, behind the scenes there were last minute efforts by Ridley's friends and relatives to secure a reprieve. One distant relative, Lord Dacre, a staunch Roman Catholic, offered Queen Mary £10,000 (a massive sum in the 1550s) if Ridley's life was spared. Latimer, by now old and ill, had no influential friends to intercede for him.

On Wednesday, 16 October 1555, Latimer and Ridley were led to the place of execution in a ditch near Balliol College, just outside the city walls. Ridley came first, wearing a black furred gown and a pair of slippers. Frail Latimer followed, wearing shabby clothes and a handkerchief round his head, joking about the slowness of his progress. They passed Cranmer's prison on their way to the stake and hoped to say farewell to their old friend, but he was busy debating theology with De Soto. At the stake Ridley and Latimer joyfully embraced—they had not met face to face since their weeks together in the Bocardo in March 1554. Ridley encouraged his fellow martyr: 'Be of good heart, brother, for God will either assuage the fury of the flame or else strengthen us to abide it.' Ridley kissed the stake and the two men prayed together, kneeling side by side.

A large number of spectators gathered to witness the execution, including the Vice Chancellor, the mayor and other dignitaries. Armed soldiers were out in force because the authorities feared trouble from the crowd.

Dr Richard Smith, a local Oxford clergyman, preached for fifteen minutes from a makeshift pulpit on the predictable text: 'If I yield my body to be burned, but have not love, I gain nothing' (1 Corinthians 13:3). The preacher exhorted Latimer and Ridley to return to the Roman Catholic Church and explained to the crowd that because they refused to recant and receive the queen's pardon they were not martyrs but suicides. Latimer and Ridley appealed to Lord Williams, the High Sheriff of Oxfordshire who was in charge of the execution, for permission to reply to Smith but were told they could only speak if it was to recant. Ridley replied, 'So long as the breath is in my body, I will never deny my Lord Christ and his truth. God's will be done in me.' In a loud voice he shouted out that he committed his cause to God.

Ridley gave away his outer clothing and a few small mementos to the officers and his weeping friends and relatives. Latimer simply allowed the officials to undress him and stood at the stake in his shirt. They were chained to the stake, back to back, and exhorted each other with earnest prayers. Shipside was allowed within the cordon of guards to give a bag of gunpowder to the two men to shorten their sufferings, which they accepted thankfully as a token of the mercy of God. As the fire was lit, Latimer encouraged his fellow martyr: 'Be of good comfort, Master Ridley, and play the man. We shall this day light such a candle, by God's grace, in England, as I trust shall never be put out.'

Latimer died swiftly and comparatively painlessly. He held out his hands into the flames and was soon overcome by the smoke. Ridley, however, suffered excruciating agony. As the flames began to rise, he called out (first in Latin, then in English): 'Into your hands, O Lord, I commit my spirit.' Yet the fire on his side of the stake burned slowly. The bundles of wood and reeds were packed so tightly that the flames burned only his feet and legs, and he cried out: 'I cannot burn'. Shipside ran forward and unwittingly made matters worse by piling on more bundles of wood high up around Ridley's face and head. This only deadened the fire still further. The martyr's legs were burned off, while above the waist he was untouched. Still conscious, he shouted out, 'For God's sake, let

Opposite this point near the Cross in the middle of Broad Street HUGH LATIMER one time Bishop of Worcester, NICHOLAS RIDLEY Bishop of London and THOMAS CRANMER Archbishop of Canterbury, were burnt for their faith in 1555 and 1556.

Above: Ridley and Latimer at the stake, from Foxe's Book of Martyrs

Facing page: A memorial plaque near the place of the execution

the fire come to me! I cannot burn! Lord, have mercy on me!' One of the soldiers eventually pulled away a bundle of wood, allowing the flames to rise. Ridley was able to swing himself forward, so that the fire reached the bag of gunpowder around his neck.

One spectator, Julius Palmer, a fellow of Magdalen College, was converted to Christ through witnessing Ridley's torments in the fire. In the days of King Edward VI he had mocked the Reformation, but now he began to denounce the persecution of Protestants as 'barbarous' and 'raging cruelty'. Palmer accepted Protestant doctrines, was condemned as a 'heretic', and was himself burned to death just outside Newbury in July 1556.

'This unworthy right hand'

From the parapet of the Bocardo, Cranmer was forced to watch the horrifying final minutes of his brother bishops. Unlike Latimer and Ridley, who stood steadfast in the face of death, the archbishop began to waver. His courage ebbed and flowed, as he was ground down psychologically by his persecutors. Visitor after visitor urged him to avoid death and return to the Roman Catholic Church. After De Soto, came another young Spanish Dominican friar, John de Garcina, recently appointed Regius Professor of Divinity. He and the prisoner held lengthy debates about papal supremacy and the doctrine of purgatory. One of Cranmer's sisters, a devout Roman Catholic and former nun, also arrived in Oxford in December 1555, intent on changing her opinions. Her method was in stark contrast to the harsh treatment by prison wardens or the aggressive interrogation by theological opponents which the archbishop had endured for twenty months. Instead she aimed gently to coax her brother. He was moved from his grim cell in the Bocardo to the comfortable home of Dr Richard Marshall, Dean of Christ Church and Vice Chancellor of the University. There Cranmer was allowed to dine with the Canons of the Cathedral, walk in the gardens and even play bowls on the lawn. He was given a tantalising reminder of his former freedom and friendships.

In the new year, Cranmer was suddenly returned to prison. The Pope had considered the report from his delegation which had examined the archbishop in September and confirmed its sentence of condemnation. In Rome, Cranmer's effigy was burned. Instructions were sent for the archbishop to be deposed and degraded. His resistance now began visibly to crumble. Under extreme stress, his steadfastness broke. He was lonely, tired, worn down, bewildered and often in tears. Cranmer grew to depend heavily on the companionship of the Bocardo's governor, Nicholas Woodson, who persistently urged recantation and threatened to leave him in total isolation if he did not submit. Late one night, towards the end of January 1556, with his spirits at their lowest ebb, Cranmer signed his first recantation. A few days later he signed a second, submitting himself to the Roman Catholic Church and the authority of the Pope. Then on 14 February, despite his recantations, Cranmer suffered the ritual humiliation of degradation in Christ Church Cathedral by Bishop Bonner of London and Bishop Thirlby of Ely, a former chaplain to the archbishop and an old friend. This was the last time he would leave the Bocardo until the day of his death. Meanwhile, under further pressure from De Soto and De Garcina, Cranmer's Protestant views completely evaporated. By the middle of March he had signed six separate recantations, repenting of his 'heretical' and 'schismatic' opinions, anathematizing Martin

Left: The Great Quadrangle of Christ Church (now known as 'Tom Quad') is the largest in Oxford

Facing page: The cross in the road, on the supposed site of the stake where the Oxford martyrs died

Luther and Ulrich Zwingli, acknowledging the Pope to be the vicar of Christ, and assenting to the doctrines of purgatory and transubstantiation. He asked for sacramental absolution and heard the Roman Catholic mass, celebrated specially for him in prison. The reformed teaching to which Cranmer had dedicated his life was now in tatters.

Queen Mary decided that even though her arch-enemy had recanted, his execution should still go ahead. He would be burned, despite obvious contradictions, as a penitent heretic. Saturday, 21 March, was decreed to be the date for Cranmer's death. He spent much of the previous day writing a speech to be delivered at the stake and discussing it with his Spanish advisers. After a final evening meal (spice cakes, bread, fruit, nuts and stewed prunes) the archbishop slept soundly. He woke to a rainy Saturday morning, which meant the speeches before his execution were transferred from outdoors to the University Church. Cranmer bade farewell to his prison guards and processed to St Mary's, flanked by De Soto and De Garcina reciting psalms antiphonally. The church was packed with an excited crowd and the prisoner was led to a specially prepared platform. Dr Henry Cole, Provost of Eton, preached a sermon rejoicing in the archbishop's conversion and promising him requiem masses for the repose of his soul. Cranmer listened to the sermon with tears rolling down his cheeks and was then invited by Cole to testify to his faith.

After a brief prayer, Cranmer began to exhort the congregation. He told them of 'the great thing which so much troubles my conscience, more than anything that I ever did or said in my whole life'. The authorities were following his written text and

Above: '*And as for the Pope, I refuse him as Christ's enemy and antichrist...*'

knew what to expect—a denunciation of his own reformed writings, followed by a declaration of his belief in transubstantiation. Yet suddenly, to their alarm, they realized that Cranmer was departing from his script. The writings which he was renouncing were in fact his various recantations, 'contrary to the truth which I thought in my heart, and written for fear of death'. The crowd was astonished. The officials were enraged. His Spanish confessors were stunned. Pandemonium broke out in the church. Through the din Cranmer continued to shout out, 'And as for the Pope, I refuse him as Christ's enemy and antichrist with all his false doctrines.' As chaos ensued, the archbishop was pulled from the platform and dragged through the streets of Oxford to the spot where Latimer and Ridley had suffered six months before.

The spectators quickly caught up with the execution party. There was little time for farewells. Cranmer was stripped to his shirt and chained to the stake. In the commotion at St Mary's, he had promised that his right hand would be the first to burn, for 'writing contrary to my heart'. Now as the fire began to take hold, Cranmer stretched out his hand into the flames for all to see, crying loudly: 'This unworthy right hand ... this hand has offended.' Although it was a wet morning, the fire burned fiercely and the archbishop died quickly with the words of Stephen on his lips: 'Lord Jesus, receive my spirit. ... I see the heavens open and Jesus standing at the right hand of God.'

Left: Cranmer at the stake, from Foxe's Book of Martyrs

The Ashmolean Museum of Art and Archaeology

The Ashmolean,
Beaumont Street, Oxford
www.ashmol.ox.ac.uk
☎ 01865 278000

The Ashmolean Museum

Founded in 1683, the Ashmolean is Britain's oldest public museum. The original collection was presented to the University of Oxford by Elias Ashmole and first situated on Broad Street. It moved to its present site in the 1890s, where it joined the University's art collections, housed in handsome neo-classical galleries. On display in the Tradescant Gallery are a stump of wood reputed to be the remains of the stake, and 'Cranmer's Band', a hinged iron hoop said to have been worn around the waist by the archbishop during his imprisonment in Oxford.

Christ Church, Oxford

Christ Church, St Aldates, Oxford
www.chch.ox.ac.uk
☎ 01865 276150

Christ Church is the largest college in Oxford. It was originally founded in 1525 by Cardinal Wolsey as 'Cardinal College', but was re-founded in 1546 by Henry VIII as 'Christ Church'. John Owen was later dean here in the 1650s. The college chapel is also the cathedral for the diocese of Oxford, one of the smallest cathedrals in England. It was once the church of St Frideswide's priory, which was established on the site in the 8th century by Oxford's patron saint.

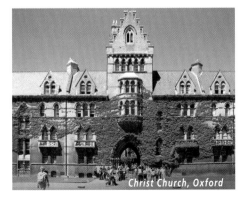

Christ Church, Oxford

Left: 'Cranmer's Pillar' at St Mary the Virgin Church. It was cut away to allow for the building of a low platform on which Cranmer made his final submission

The Divinity School (the Bodleian Library)

The Bodleian Library, Broad Street, Oxford
www.bodley.ox.ac.uk
☎ 01865 277000

St Mary the Virgin (the University Church)

St Mary the Virgin, High Street, Oxford
www.university-church.ox.ac.uk
☎ 01865 279111

There has probably been a church on this site since Anglo-Saxon times, standing in the physical centre of the old walled city of Oxford. As the University grew up around it, the church became, by the 13th century, the seat of university government and a centre for academic debate. Many famous sermons have been preached here by men such as John Wesley, John Keble and C. S. Lewis. There are good views of the city from the tower.

St Michael at the North Gate (the City Church)

St Michael at the North Gate, Cornmarket, Oxford
www.smng.org.uk
☎ 01865 240940

Built during the late Saxon period around 1040, the tower of St Michael at the North Gate is Oxford's oldest surviving building. There are good views of the city from the roof. There is a small museum in the tower, where the martyrs' cell door from the old Bocardo prison is on display.

The Divinity School is the oldest University (as opposed to college) building in Oxford, begun in the 1420s though not finished until the 1480s. It is entered through the Old Schools Quadrangle with its Great Gate, also known as 'The Tower of the Five Orders of Architecture'. The Divinity School was initially used for theology lectures and debates, but is now part of the Bodleian Library. The surrounding Bodleian buildings were begun in 1610 at the bequest of former Oxford student, Thomas Bodley. It is now the second largest library in the country, after the British Library in London.

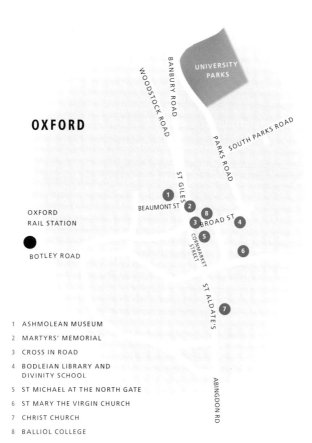

OXFORD

BANBURY ROAD

WOODSTOCK ROAD

UNIVERSITY PARKS

SOUTH PARKS ROAD

PARKS ROAD

ST GILES

BEAUMONT ST

OXFORD RAIL STATION

BOTLEY ROAD

BROAD ST

CORNMARKET STREET

ST ALDATE'S

ABINGDON RD

1   ASHMOLEAN MUSEUM

2   MARTYRS' MEMORIAL

3   CROSS IN ROAD

4   BODLEIAN LIBRARY AND DIVINITY SCHOOL

5   ST MICHAEL AT THE NORTH GATE

6   ST MARY THE VIRGIN CHURCH

7   CHRIST CHURCH

8   BALLIOL COLLEGE

Left: Detail from the Oxford martyrs' memorial, representing the martyrs' temporary suffering and eternal victory—a crown of thorns and a crown of glory

Right: The pelican, an ancient symbol of martyrdom, was part of Cranmer's coat of arms

of the first martyrs at Canterbury on 12 July 1555.

Three others were burned alongside Bland. One was a local man, Nicholas Shetterden, who was imprisoned for many months in Canterbury's Westgate for preaching Protestant doctrines. His wealthy brother offered to bestow a large fortune upon him if he would recant, but the martyr replied that he was looking for an eternal reward. In a farewell letter to his mother, the day before his death, Shetterden pleaded with her to 'beware of the great idolatry and the blasphemous mass', and to follow God's word, trusting in Christ alone for salvation. He signed and sealed the letter with his own blood and added a postscript: 'Appointed to be slain for Christ's cause and the maintenance of his most sound and true religion.'

Before Mary's reign was over, forty-one Protestants were burned to death at Canterbury. Few of

Above: The Canterbury martyrs' memorial, erected in 1899 on Martyrs Field Road (detail below)

those who suffered lived in the city itself, but they were brought there from the surrounding towns and villages. One such was Alice Benden from Staplehurst. She was imprisoned for a fortnight for refusing to attend mass in her local church, describing it as 'idolatry committed against the glory of God'. Once released, her husband tried to force her to mass, but she remained immovable. He then cruelly offered to pay for his wife to be taken back to prison, so she gave herself up to avoid this additional humiliation. Alice was condemned to death by the Bishop of Dover and thrown into 'Monday's Hole', a small underground vault at Canterbury, where she had to sleep on straw and go nine weeks without changing her clothes. Because she annoyed her gaolers by insisting on singing psalms, she was eventually moved to the Westgate and then to Canterbury Castle, before being led with six others to execution.

Above: The Westgate, the old gaol for the city of Canterbury, next to Holy Cross Church

Five martyrs also starved to death in Canterbury Castle before they could be taken to the stake. Amongst them was Alice Potkins, who when asked her age replied, 'I am forty-nine years according to my old life, but only one year old since I believed in Christ.' Interrogated by the authorities, she insisted: 'I am resolved never to confess to a priest, nor pray to a saint, not creep to the cross.' When Alice starved to death, her body was thrown out and buried in the highway.

A sign of God's favour

While the fires raged at Canterbury, Protestants continued to suffer elsewhere across Kent. There were also burnings at Ashford, Dartford, Maidstone, Rochester, Tonbridge and Wye. One of those to suffer was Christopher Wade, a linen weaver from Dartford. He was arrested in June 1555 and condemned to death by Maurice Griffith, Bishop of Rochester. On 17 July, Wade was taken to a gravel pit near the river Brent for execution. Many spectators gathered from the surrounding villages to witness the event and local fruiterers did a brisk trade selling cherries from their horse-drawn carts. As they reached the spot, Margery Polley (a widow and fellow prisoner) encouraged the martyr: 'You may rejoice to see such a crowd gathered to celebrate your marriage today.' Wade stripped off

Above: Carver's brewery in Brighton, now the Black Lion Pub

Below: A memorial plaque to Carver

and tossed it out to the crowd. Yet the sheriff ordered on pain of death that it be thrown back to be burned with him. Carver exhorted the gathered crowd to resist the teaching of the Pope and hold fast to the biblical gospel. He proclaimed, 'Brothers and sisters, witness all of you that I have come to seal Christ's Gospel with my blood, because I know that it is true. It has been truly preached here in Lewes, and in all places in England, and now is not. And because I will not deny God's Gospel, and be obedient to man's laws, I am condemned to die.' The sheriff retorted that those who did not follow the Pope were damned, and challenged Carver: 'Speak to your God, that he may deliver you now or else strike me down as an example for the

condemned and sent back to Sussex for punishment. Rather than being executed together, the authorities thought it would have a more salutary effect on the local populace if they were burned in three different towns along the south coast.

DERYK CARVER
FIRST PROTESTANT MARTYR
BURNT AT LEWES JULY 22ND 1555.
LIVED IN THIS BREWERY.

RECONSTRUCTED 1974

people.' As the flames rose around the Protestant, he leapt up and down, and prayed out loud: 'O Lord my God, you have written that he who will not forsake wife, children, house, and everything he has and take up his cross and follow you, is not worthy of you. But you Lord know that I have forsaken all to come to you. Lord have mercy on me, for to you I commend my spirit and my soul rejoices in you.' He left behind five orphaned children.

The first to die was Deryk Carver at Lewes. On 22 July 1555, he was taken to a stake set up outside the Star Inn, in the centre of town. A barrel was prepared for the martyr to stand in and his English Bible was contemptuously thrown in too. Carver climbed into the barrel, picked up the Bible

Above: *Steyning parish church, built in the 11th century, has a distinctive 'chequer' design on the tower. On nearby Chantry Green John Launder was burned*

The next day, 23 July, John Launder was burned at Steyning, on the small Chantry Green close to the parish church. On 24 July his friend, Thomas Iveson, was burned at Chichester, probably in the precincts of the cathedral. So died the first of the Sussex martyrs. They were followed within a year by others at Lewes, Chichester, East Grinstead and Mayfield.

Hidden, but hunted

Richard Woodman, who lived in the village of Warbleton near Heathfield, is the best known of the Sussex martyrs. He was a farmer and iron manufacturer, employing a hundred workers while still in his twenties. He was also churchwarden of his local

parish church of St Mary's, and a convinced Protestant.

The rector of Warbleton, George Fairbanke, had been a supporter of the Reformation under Edward VI but changed his tune when Mary Tudor came to the throne. One Sunday in the spring of 1554 he preached that forgiveness of sins is obtained through receiving the sacraments. This was too much for Woodman, who stood up and publicly rebuked his rector for recanting his reformed beliefs. The churchwarden was arrested and sent to the King's Bench prison in Southwark (alongside Taylor, Ferrar, Bradford and Philpot) where he was held for a year and nine months. He was told he would be burned, but was mysteriously released in December 1555, on the very day Archdeacon Philpot was martyred at Smithfield.

Woodman returned to Sussex to his iron business and in his spare time began to preach the gospel from place to place. The High Sheriff, Sir John Gage, was informed and a warrant was again issued for Woodman's capture. Early one morning, while Woodman was ploughing his field, three officers arrived to arrest him. He co-operated, asking only to be allowed first to go home, to change his clothes and eat his breakfast. It was then discovered that the officers had forgotten to bring the arrest warrant, so Woodman refused to budge any further. While they went to fetch it he escaped from his cottage and fled to the nearby woods.

The hunt was now on. The authorities had the coast watched from Dover to Portsmouth, in fear that he would escape to France. Yet Woodman remained hiding in the woods for six or seven weeks, with his Bible and writing materials. Each day his wife brought him whatever he needed. When things quietened down, Woodman did indeed go to Flanders and France for a few weeks, but absence from his family made each day 'feel like seven years' so he returned to Sussex.

The sheriff's men continued to hunt for Woodman in Warbleton,

searching his cottage sometimes twice a week. He had built a secret hide-out in the loft, which they failed to discover. Twenty times he was at home when they arrived, but they never found him. Eventually Woodman was betrayed by his own brother, who owed him a large amount of money. One evening, at about nine o'clock, twelve of the sheriff's men surrounded his home and hid in the bushes to keep watch. Woodman was sitting on his bed when suddenly his young daughter spotted the spies and ran indoors shouting, 'Mother, mother, twenty men are coming!'

There was no time to flee, so Woodman dashed into his secret hide-out. His wife, Margery, quickly closed the front door and barred it, but the sheriff's men surrounded the house and threatened to smash the door

Above: *The Chantry Green in Steyning, where Launder was burned. The house was originally built for the priest of the local chantry, where masses were sung for the souls of the dead*

Above: Chichester Cathedral

Below: A memorial plaque to the Chichester martyrs, on the wall of Providence Chapel

FAITHFUL
UNTO
DEATH
REV. II. 10

To the memory of
THOMAS IVESON
and
RICHARD HOOK
who were martyred
at CHICHESTER 1555
for their
faith

down. She protested her husband was not at home, but they forced their way in and ransacked the house. Still unable to find the fugitive they were about to leave empty-handed once more, when they were informed about the hide-out and demanded that Mrs Woodman show them the entrance. Margery sent them into the wrong room and shouted to her husband, 'Away, away!'

Woodman had no option. He wrenched some boards from the roof above his head to escape, but the noise alerted his pursuers. He leapt from the roof and ran off down a cinder track, but without his shoes. The officers followed, with swords drawn, shouting, 'Strike him, strike him!' As Woodman turned around to see how close they were, he trod on a sharp cinder and stumbled into a muddy hole. Before he could recover, a local ruffian nicknamed Parker the Wild was upon him, quickly followed by the rest. This time

The Victorians remember the martyrs

During the early 19th century the strength of Roman Catholicism in England increased sharply. On the political scene, the movement for 'Catholic Emancipation' removed anti-catholic legislation from the statute book, culminating in the Roman Catholic Relief Act of 1829. Meanwhile, in an initiative known as the 'Papal Aggression', Pope Pius IX sent bishops to re-establish Roman Catholic dioceses in England in 1850. This was paralleled by a swing away from Reformation principles within the Church of England, which saw the rise of Tractarianism and Anglo-Catholicism.

Fearful that England's Protestant heritage would be forgotten, supporters of the Reformation began to construct memorials across the country wherever there was a connection with the martyrs of Mary Tudor. Most of these memorials were built in the period between 1840 to 1910, supported by public subscription or donated by individuals or organizations such as the Protestant Alliance.

Obelisks, crosses, plaques, stained-glass windows and even churches were erected in honour of the martyrs and as a reminder of the truths for which they died.

Pictured: *The unveiling of Lewes martyrs' memorial by the Earl of Portsmouth in 1901, in front of a crowd of nearly six thousand*

TRAVEL INFORMATION

Canterbury Cathedral

Canterbury Cathedral, Canterbury
www.canterbury-cathedral.org
☎ 01227 762862

St Augustine, the first Archbishop of Canterbury, came as a missionary to England in AD 597, sent from Rome by Pope Gregory the Great. On his arrival he was given a church at Canterbury by Ethelbert, King of Kent, whose wife, Bertha, was already a Christian. Here a monastic community lived for nearly a thousand years until it was dissolved in 1540 by Henry VIII. The king also destroyed the famous shrine to St Thomas Becket (murdered in the cathedral in 1170) to which many thousands went each year on pilgrimage. Cranmer's persecutor and successor, Cardinal Pole, is buried in the cathedral.

Canterbury Castle

Canterbury Castle, Castle Street, Canterbury
☎ 01227 378100

Canterbury Castle was one of the three original royal castles of Kent (the others being at Rochester and Dover). It was established by William the Conqueror soon after the Battle of Hastings and its massive keep (once twice the height) was built in the early 1100s by Henry I.

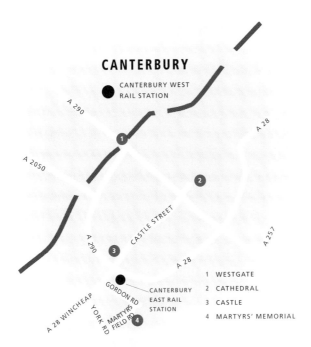

CANTERBURY

CANTERBURY WEST
RAIL STATION

A 290

A 28

①

A 2050

②

CASTLE STREET

A 257

A 290

③

A 28

GORDON RD

CANTERBURY
EAST RAIL
STATION

A 28 WINCHEAP

YORK RD

MARTYRS
FIELD RD

④

1 WESTGATE
2 CATHEDRAL
3 CASTLE
4 MARTYRS' MEMORIAL

For many centuries Canterbury Castle was used as a prison for the county of Kent. By the late 18th century it was largely a ruin and much was demolished.

Right: *A statue of Queen Elizabeth I at Canterbury Cathedral, Bible in hand*

Canterbury Westgate Museum

Canterbury Westgate Museum, St Peter's Street, Canterbury
www.canterbury-museum.co.uk
☎ 01227 789576

Canterbury's Westgate is one of the best surviving medieval gates in Britain, standing guard on the road to London. It was built in the 1370s to replace a 3rd century Roman gate and was

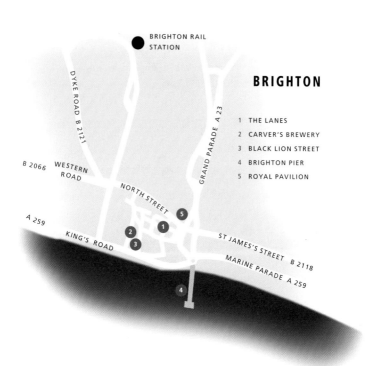

BRIGHTON

1 THE LANES
2 CARVER'S BREWERY
3 BLACK LION STREET
4 BRIGHTON PIER
5 ROYAL PAVILION

BRIGHTON RAIL STATION

DYKE ROAD B 2121

GRAND PARADE A 23

B 2066 WESTERN ROAD

NORTH STREET

A 259

KING'S ROAD

ST JAMES'S STREET B 2118

MARINE PARADE A 259

partly paid for by Archbishop Simon of Sudbury (murdered in the Peasants' Revolt of 1381). Holy Cross Church nearby was constructed at the same time, one of only a few new Kentish churches in the late 14th century. The Westgate acted as the city gaol from 1473. There is a small museum in the tower and panoramic views from the rooftop battlements.

The Lanes, Brighton

Between Brighton's Royal Pavilion and the sea stands Brighton Old Town ('Brighthelmstone'). This dense network of narrow streets and cobbled courtyards is now known as 'The Lanes'. It was burned to the ground by French raiders in 1514 but soon developed into a prosperous Tudor fishing town. Deryk Carver's brewery, established in 1546, survives in Black Lion Street. It fell into disuse and was demolished in 1968, but a replica was built with the original materials six years later.

Lewes

Every year, on the evening of 5 November, Lewes holds extravagant Bonfire Night celebrations, without parallel anywhere in the country. There are six local bonfire societies, which organize a huge torch-lit fancy-dress parade, witnessed by a crowd of tens of thousands. As well as being a massive street party, the pageant commemorates the burning of the Lewes martyrs and the discovery on 5 November 1605 of

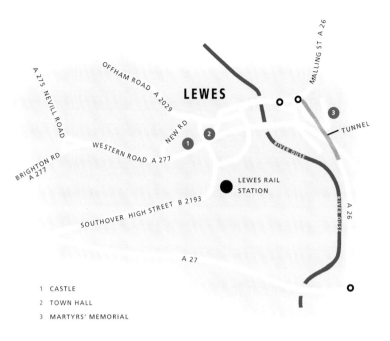

LEWES

1   CASTLE
2   TOWN HALL
3   MARTYRS' MEMORIAL

the Roman Catholic plot to blow up Parliament and kill the king. Effigies of Guy Fawkes and the Pope are burned each year. The martyrs' memorial on Cliffe Hill is a steep climb by foot and there is no access for vehicles. (For the story of Guy Fawkes see the Day One publication: *Gunpowder, treason and plot* by Clive Anderson).

Above: *Lewes Town Hall stands on the site of the Star Inn. The war memorial, in the foreground, is on the spot of the martyrdoms*

Steyning

The picturesque town of Steyning in Sussex was once a prosperous port and trading centre, but went into a lengthy period of decline in the middle ages. Today it is famous for its large number of historic buildings, with many timber-framed houses surviving from the 14th and 15th centuries. The parish church was built by the Abbey of Fécamp in Normandy, which once administered the town.

Key dates for the martyrs of Mary Tudor

6 JULY 1553
Death of King Edward VI

19 JULY 1553
Mary proclaimed queen

4 FEBRUARY 1555
John Rogers at Smithfield – p.24

8 FEBRUARY 1555
Laurence Saunders at Coventry – p.40

9 FEBRUARY 1555
Rowland Taylor at Hadleigh – p.43

John Hooper at Gloucester – p.54

26 MARCH 1555
William Hunter at Brentwood – p.67

Thomas Higbed at Horndon-on-the-Hill – p.68

Thomas Causton at Rayleigh, Essex – p.68

29 MARCH 1555
John Lawrence at Colchester – p.68

30 MARCH 1555
Robert Ferrar at Carmarthen – p.57

Rawlins White at Cardiff – p.57

24 APRIL 1555
George Marsh at Chester – p.86

30 MAY 1555
John Cardmaker and John Warne at Smithfield – p.28

1 JULY 1555
John Bradford and John Leaf at Smithfield – p.30

12 JULY 1555
John Bland, Nicholas Shetterden, and others at Canterbury – p.107

17 JULY 1555
Christopher Wade at Dartford – p.109

18 JULY 1555
Margery Polley at Tonbridge – p.110

22 JULY 1555
Deryk Carver at Lewes – p.112

23 JULY 1555
John Launder at Steyning – p.113

24 JULY 1555
Thomas Iveson at Chichester – p.113

31 AUGUST 1555
Robert Samuel at Ipswich – p.42

16 OCTOBER 1555
Hugh Latimer and Nicholas Ridley at Oxford – p.98

18 DECEMBER 1555
John Philpot at Smithfield – p.32

21 MARCH 1556
Thomas Cranmer at Oxford – p.102

5 MAY 1556
Thomas Drowry at Gloucester – p.53

15 MAY 1556
Hugh Laverock and John Apprice at Stratford-le-Bow – p.71

27 JUNE 1556
Thirteen at Stratford-le-Bow

16 JULY 1556
Julius Palmer at Newbury – p.99

22 JUNE 1557
Richard Woodman and Alexander Hosmer with eight others at Lewes – p.116

13 JULY 1557
Simon Miller and Elizabeth Cooper at Norwich – p.42

2 AUGUST 1557
Ten at Colchester, including William and Alice Munt, Rose Allen and Elizabeth Folkes – p.69

23 SEPTEMBER 1557
Cicely Ormes at Norwich – p.42

22 DECEMBER 1557
John Rough at Smithfield– p.32

28 MARCH 1558
Cuthbert Symson at Smithfield – p.33

27 JUNE 1558
Seven including Roger Holland at Smithfield – p.33

28 JUNE 1558
Six at Brentford – p.33

10 JULY 1558
Richard Yeoman at Norwich – p.44

4 NOVEMBER 1558
Alice Driver at Ipswich – p.42

Agnes Prest at Exeter – p.116

10 NOVEMBER 1558
Five at Canterbury – p.116

17 NOVEMBER 1558
Death of Queen Mary and Cardinal Pole

15 JANUARY 1559
Coronation of Queen Elizabeth

MEMORIALS TO PROTESTANT MARTYRS IN ENGLAND AND WALES

Berkshire

NEWBURY

Newbury

Memorial to Christopher Shoemaker (burned 1518), Julius Palmer and two other martyrs (burned 1556) on Enbourne Road

Bristol

BRISTOL

Tablets to five martyrs (burned 1555-57) at St Saviour and St Mary's Church, Cotham (formerly Highbury Congregational Chapel); statue of William Tyndale (martyred 1536) in Millennium Square

Buckinghamshire

AMERSHAM

Obelisk to eleven Lollard martyrs (burned 1506-32) on a hill overlooking the town

CHESHAM

Memorial cross to Thomas Harding (burned 1532) in St Mary's churchyard, Church Street

Amersham

Cambridgeshire

CAMBRIDGE

Tablet to Thomas Bilney (burned 1531), Robert Barnes (burned 1540), and Hugh Latimer (burned 1555) in St Edward the Martyr Church.

Cheshire

CHESTER

Obelisk to George Marsh (burned 1555) near St Paul's Church, Boughton and a tablet in St John the Baptist Church, Little St John's Street

Devon

EXETER

Obelisk to Thomas Benet (burned 1531) and Agnes Prest (burned 1557) on the corner of Denmark Road and Barnfield Road

East Sussex

BRIGHTON

Tablet to Deryk Carver (burned 1555) in Black Lion Street

HEATHFIELD

Obelisk to four martyrs (burned 1557) outside Heathfield Chapel, Punnetts Town

LEWES

Obelisk to seventeen martyrs (burned 1555-57) on Cliffe Hill and a tablet on the Town Hall

MAYFIELD

Monument to seven martyrs (burned 1556-57) in the grounds of Colkins Mill Church (formerly Mayfield Congregational Chapel)

WARBLETON

Memorial to Richard Woodman (burned 1557) in St Mary's churchyard

Essex

BRENTWOOD

Obelisk to William Hunter (burned 1555) on the corner of Shenfield Road and Ingrave Road

COLCHESTER

Tablet to twenty-three martyrs (burned 1555-58) in St Peter's Church, North Hill; tablet to twenty-nine martyrs (burned or died in prison 1428-1664) in the Town Hall

GREAT DUNMOW

Tablet to Thomas Bowyer (burned 1556) on Bowyer's Bridge, Thaxted Road

HORDON-ON-THE-HILL

Tablet to Thomas Higbed (burned 1555) in St Peter and St Paul's Church

RAYLEIGH

Obelisk to Thomas Causton and John Ardingley (burned 1555) on the High Street

SAFFRON WALDEN

Tablet to John Newman (burned 1555) on the Town Hall

Gloucestershire

GLOUCESTER

Monument to John Hooper (burned 1555) in St Mary's Square and a memorial window in Gloucester Cathedral

NORTH NIBLEY

Tower to William Tyndale on a hill overlooking the village

Right: Memorial tablet on Rochester Baptist Church

North Nibley

Above: *The tallest martyrs' memorial is the monument to William Tyndale on Nibley Knoll, erected in 1865, which stands 111 feet (34 metres) high*

SLIMBRIDGE

Screen to William Tyndale in St John's Church

Hertfordshire

ST ALBANS

Tablet to George Tankerfield (burned 1555) near the abbey gateway

Kent

CANTERBURY

Memorial cross to forty-one martyrs (burned 1555-58) on Martyrs Field Road

DARTFORD

Memorial to Christopher Wade, Nicholas Hall and Margery Polley (burned 1555) at St Edmund's Pleasance (formerly East Hill cemetery)

HERNE

Statue of Nicholas Ridley (burned 1555) in St Martin's Church

PEMBURY

Drinking trough to Margery Polley on Pembury Green.

ROCHESTER

Tablet to Nicholas Ridley and to three Rochester martyrs (burned 1555-56) at Rochester Baptist Church, Crow Lane

STAPLEHURST

Monument to five local martyrs (burned or died in prison 1556-57) at Cuckold's Corner

Lancashire

BOLTON

Memorial cross to George Marsh (burned 1555) in Deane parish churchyard; also a memorial window and a carving on the Lord's Table, inside the church

London

CITY OF LONDON

Tablet to John Rogers, John Bradford and John Philpot (all burned 1555) and other Smithfield martyrs, on the wall of St Bartholomew's Hospital, Smithfield; bust of William Tyndale at St Dunstan-in-the-West, Fleet Street

CLERKENWELL

Plaque to sixty-six Smithfield martyrs (burned 1400-1558) in St James' Church, Clerkenwell Close

SOUTHWARK

Statue of John Rogers in Southwark Cathedral

STRATFORD-LE-BOW

Memorial to twenty-two martyrs (burned 1555-56) in St John's churchyard, Stratford Broadway

WESTMINSTER

Statue of William Tyndale in Victoria Embankment Gardens and a tablet in Westminster Abbey

Norfolk

BECCLES

Tablet to three martyrs (burned 1556) at Beccles Baptist Church, Station Road

NORWICH

Tablet to Thomas Bilney (burned 1531) at the Guildhall, and to other local martyrs at The Bridge House pub, Riverside Road (site of the Lollards' Pit)

Oxfordshire

OXFORD

Memorial cross to Hugh Latimer, Nicholas Ridley and Thomas Cranmer (burned 1555-56) on St Giles and a tablet on Broad Street; memorial window of William Tyndale in Hertford College Chapel

Staffordshire

LICHFIELD

Tablets to three Protestant martyrs (burned 1555-57) at St Mary's Church, Market Square

Suffolk

BURY ST EDMUNDS

Pillar to seventeen martyrs (burned or died in prison 1555-58) near the cathedral

HADLEIGH

Unhewn stone and obelisk to Rowland Taylor (burned 1555) in a field outside the town; memorial window and tablet in St Mary's Church

IPSWICH

Pillar to nine martyrs (burned 1538-58) in Christchurch Park

LAXFIELD

Tablet to John Noyes (burned 1555) at Laxfield Baptist Church, High Street

Warwickshire

MANCETTER

Tablets to Robert Glover (burned 1555) and Joyce Lewis (burned 1557) in St Peter's Church

West Midlands

BIRMINGHAM

Tablet to John Rogers (burned 1555) on the High Street, Deritend; bust of Rogers at St Peter and St Paul's Church, Witton Road, Aston

Coventry

COVENTRY

Cross to Laurence Saunders and ten other Coventry martyrs (burned 1510-55) on Quinton Road (site of the Hollows). There is also a mosaic of the martyrs in Broadgate House

West Sussex

CHICHESTER

Tablet to Thomas Iveson and Richard Hook (burned 1555) at Providence Chapel, Chapel Street

EAST GRINSTEAD

Memorial slabs to three martyrs (burned 1556) in St Swithun's churchyard

STEYNING

Tablet to John Launder (burned 1555) near the Chantry Green

WEST HOATHLY

Memorial slabs to the East Grinstead martyrs

WILLIAM COBERLEY
JOHN MAUNDREL
JOHN SPICER

WHO WERE BURNED AT THE STAKE IN SALISBURY
ON 24 MARCH 1556

"for the word of God and for the testimony of Jesus Christ"
REV. 1. 9.
"Be thou faithful unto death, and I will give thee a crown of life"
REV. 2.10.

Above: *Tablet to the Salisbury martyrs, erected in 1993*

Tablet to Anne Tree (burned 1556) in St Margaret's Church

West Yorkshire

HALIFAX

Canopied tomb to Robert Ferrar (burned 1555) in St John the Baptist Church, Church Street

Wiltshire

SALISBURY

Tablets to three martyrs (burned 1556) in St Paul's Church, Fisherton Street and on Malmesbury House, the Cathedral Close

Wales

CARDIFF

Tablet to Rawlins White (burned 1555) in Howells Department Store (formerly Bethany Baptist Church) and a statue in St John's Church, near Cardiff Castle

CARMARTHEN

Tablets to Robert Ferrar in St Peter's Church, St Peter's Street and at Nott Square

HAVERFORDWEST

Column to William Nichol (burned 1558) on the High Street

Guernsey

ST PETER PORT

Tablet to three martyrs and a new born infant (burned 1556) halfway up Tower Hill Steps

The author and publisher would be pleased to hear of any other Protestant martyrs' memorials known to readers.

THE MARTYRS OF MARY TUDOR IN ENGLAND AND WALES

SOME KEY LOCATIONS

1 Lancaster
2 Bolton
3 Chester
4 Carmarthen
5 Cardiff
6 Gloucester
7 Coventry

8 Oxford
9 Exeter
10 Chichester
11 Steyning
12 Brighton
13 Lewes
14 Warbleton

15 Pembury
16 Tonbridge
17 Canterbury
18 Dartford
19 London
20 Brentwood
21 Colchester

22 Ipswich
23 Hadleigh
24 Lavenham
25 Bury St
    Edmunds
26 Norwich

FURTHER READING

John Foxe's, *Book of Martyrs*.
The classic martyrology, often reprinted in abridged form.

Jasper Ridley, *Bloody Mary's Martyrs* (London: Robinson, 2001)
A lively account of all two hundred and eighty-three Marian martyrs, in chronological order.

J. C. Ryle, *Five English Reformers* (1890; republished Edinburgh: Banner of Truth, 1960)
A passionate reminder of the truths for which the reformers were burned.

For details of the British Academy's 'John Foxe Project', scholarly research into Foxe's *Book of Martyrs*, see www.shef.ac.uk/hri/foxe.htm.

ACKNOWLEDGEMENTS

For photographs of Chichester, East Grinstead, Lewes, Pembury and West Hoathly I am grateful to Ruth and Hugh Atherstone pp 111, 115, 121, 126.
Images of items from Gloucester pp 50, 55, 56, 60 copyright Gloucester Folk Museum.
Image of Brentwood Martyr's Tree p 65 courtesy Essex Record Office.
Image of Colchester Moot Hall p 72 courtesy Colchester Local Studies Library.
Photograph of Smithills Hall p 77 copyright Smithills Hall and Park Trust.
Photographs of Lancaster Castle pp 79, 81 copyright Lancashire County Council.
Images of Chester's old Northgate and George Marsh at the stake pp 84, 85 courtesy Chester History and Heritage, Chester City Council.
Image of the Oxford Bocardo p 91 copyright Oxfordshire County Council Photographic Archive.
Various images of Protestants pp 15, 102, 116, 118, courtesy the Protestant Alliance.
All other photographs are by the author.

AUTHOR

Dr Andrew Atherstone was educated at Christ's College, Cambridge and Wycliffe Hall, Oxford. He is an Anglican minister and has worked for churches in Islington, Reading and Oxfordshire. His main research interest is the history of Anglican Evangelicalism. Andrew is married to Catherine and they have a young family.